Systems Thinking

*An AI's Guide to 100 Ways to Spot
Connections Humans Often Overlook*

Table of Contents

Introduction:
Seeing What Others Miss

Imagine a web stretched out before you. Some threads are easy to see — clear, bold, and obvious. But others fade into the background, quietly shaping everything around them. Most people focus only on the visible threads, missing the deeper interconnections that truly define the system. Systems thinking is about stepping back to see the whole web — how everything interacts, influences, and evolves together.

This book is your guide to systems thinking, a mindset and a skillset that will forever change the way you approach problems. With it, you'll learn to think beyond isolated parts and surface-level causes, uncovering the structures, flows, and forces that drive the bigger picture. By mastering these insights, you'll discover how to make smarter decisions, anticipate ripple effects, and design solutions that truly last.

Who This Book Is For

This book is for problem-solvers, innovators, leaders, and lifelong learners. It's for anyone who looks at the world and knows there's more going on than meets the eye. Whether you're leading a team, analyzing complex challenges, or simply trying to make better decisions in your own life, systems thinking will unlock a new level of understanding.

From business professionals navigating intricate organizations to environmentalists tackling global challenges, systems thinking is the missing tool for seeing clearly in a complex world. Even if you've never thought of yourself as "analytical" or "technical," this book will guide you step-by-step in discovering how to see the unseen and connect the dots others miss.

Why Systems Thinking Matters

The challenges of society are systemic by nature. They aren't caused by one single thing, nor can they be solved by simple fixes. Whether it's an environmental issue, an organizational bottleneck, or a personal challenge, problems exist in interconnected webs.

Systems thinking offers clarity in this chaos. It equips you to see the underlying structures that drive behavior and outcomes. Once you can do that, you'll find opportunities for change that others overlook. This isn't just about solving problems; it's about transforming how you think, act, and create.

What You'll Gain

With this book, you'll learn how to:

- Recognize the unseen interconnections that influence your world.
- Uncover root causes instead of reacting to surface-level symptoms.
- Design solutions that work sustainably, not just temporarily.
- Make smarter, faster decisions by focusing on the right leverage points.

More importantly, you'll gain a mindset that shifts the way you see everything — from the systems in nature and society to the systems in your own daily life. It's a new lens for understanding the world.

Part 1: The Basics of Seeing Systems

Understanding systems starts with how you see them. In this section, you'll learn to step back, identify relationships, and recognize the structures that shape the world around you. These foundational skills will open your eyes to connections and influences you may never have noticed before, giving you the clarity to analyze problems and opportunities in a whole new way.

Chapter 1: Zoom Out to See the Big Picture

The Power of Perspective

To solve any problem effectively, you need to resist the urge to focus solely on what's immediately in front of you. Zooming out allows you to see how smaller pieces fit into a larger whole, revealing connections and influences that would otherwise remain invisible. Without this broader perspective, you risk treating symptoms instead of addressing root causes.

How to Zoom Out

1. **Start with Context:** Ask yourself, "What system is this problem a part of?" Instead of isolating an issue, consider how it fits into a larger environment or network.

2. **Use Visual Tools:** Sketch diagrams or maps of how various components interact within the system. This can help highlight overlooked connections.

3. **Shift Between Levels:** Alternate between granular details and the broader picture, asking, "How does this piece contribute to the system as a whole?"
4. **Ask Systemic Questions:** Replace "What's wrong?" with "What external factors influence this situation?" and "What ripple effects might this create?"

Real-World Example

Imagine a city facing frequent power outages. A narrow view might blame aging infrastructure. However, zooming out reveals a more complex web of factors: population growth, poor urban planning, and resource mismanagement. Addressing the infrastructure alone would miss the broader, systemic causes. By zooming out, city planners can tackle root issues, such as demand forecasting or improving resource allocation.

Why It Matters

Zooming out empowers you to see the world as an interconnected whole. It prevents you from getting stuck on immediate symptoms and instead focuses your attention on systemic drivers of change. This shift in perspective is the first and most essential step toward becoming a systems thinker.

Exercises

1. **Map the Bigger Picture:** Think of a current challenge in your life — personal, professional, or societal. Sketch a diagram showing how it connects to other areas, such as people, resources, or external forces. Reflect on what might be influencing the problem beyond its immediate context.
2. **Zoom Out Physically:** Go to a high point in your neighborhood — a hill, a tall building, or even an aerial photo online. Observe the broader environment and think about how what you see (roads, traffic, green spaces) might influence specific events, like traffic jams or neighborhood dynamics.
3. **Ask Three Why's:** For any problem, ask yourself, "Why is this happening?" three times, each time moving further away from the surface issue. For example: "Why is my

team missing deadlines? Because tasks aren't clear. Why aren't tasks clear? Because we lack a process for assigning roles. Why do we lack a process? Because we haven't discussed priorities as a group."

Key Takeaway

The bigger picture often holds the true solution. Zooming out helps you see it.

Chapter 2: Identify Key Stakeholders

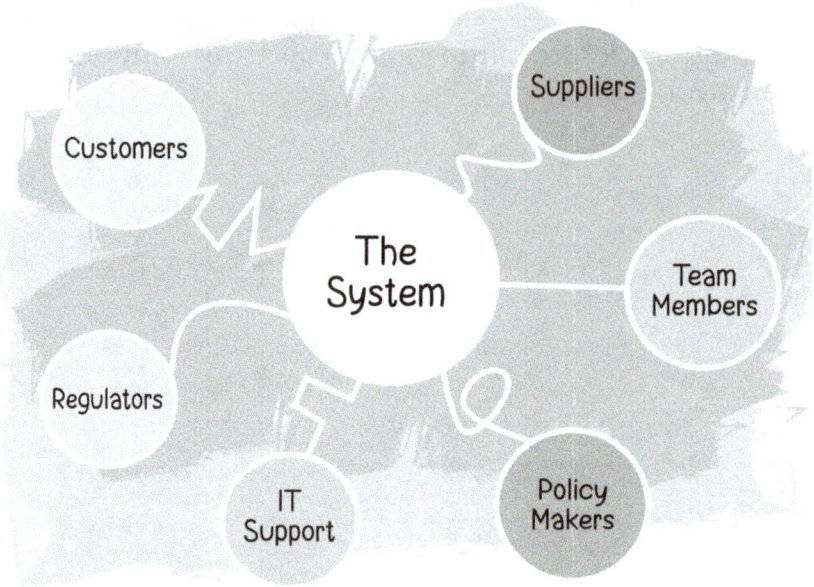

The Stakeholders Difference

In every system, there are individuals, groups, or entities that influence or are influenced by its behavior. These are the stakeholders, and understanding their roles is critical for grasping how the system functions. Stakeholders are the threads that hold the system together. Missing even one important stakeholder can cause you to misinterpret a system's problems, overlook potential solutions, or make changes that backfire.

Take a workplace environment as an example. If you're trying to boost team productivity, the obvious stakeholders might seem to be just the team members themselves. But by looking deeper, you'll uncover other crucial players: managers who set expectations, clients whose demands affect workloads, and even the IT team maintaining the tools your staff relies on. Identifying all stakeholders ensures your approach is grounded in the full complexity of the system.

How to Identify Key Stakeholders

1. **Outline Influencers and Impacted Parties:** Start by asking two questions:
   - Who has the power to affect the system?
   - Who is affected by the system's outcomes?

     Use this to create a simple map or list.

2. **Classify Relationships:** Not all stakeholders play the same role. Some actively shape the system (e.g. leaders, regulators), while others are recipients of its outputs (e.g. customers, employees). Distinguish between decision-makers, participants, and bystanders.

3. **Trace Connections:** Explore how stakeholders interact with each other. For example, how do employee needs align — or conflict — with organizational goals? Are suppliers working in harmony with logistical systems? This reveals the system's dynamics.

4. **Listen and Learn:** Engage with stakeholders directly. What are their needs, concerns, and priorities? Their perspectives may reveal blind spots in your understanding.

Real-World Example

Consider the development of a new public park. At first glance, the stakeholders might seem obvious: the local government funding it and the residents who will use it. But with a deeper dive, additional players emerge: environmental organizations concerned about preserving green spaces, businesses that could benefit from increased foot traffic, and construction teams tasked with building the park.

By identifying and understanding these diverse stakeholders, planners can anticipate challenges, balance competing interests, and ensure long-term success.

Why It Matters

Ignoring key stakeholders leads to incomplete solutions. Imagine redesigning a public transportation system while overlooking the needs of low-income communities who rely on it most. Or implementing a workplace policy without consulting the very employees it affects. Recognizing stakeholders ensures your decisions account for the system's complexity, making them more effective and sustainable.

Exercises

1. **Stakeholder Structure:** Choose a challenge you're working on and make a list of everyone it impacts or involves. Next, draw a diagram showing how these stakeholders interact with one another and the system itself.

2. **Role Reversal Exercise:** Pick one stakeholder and write down the problem from their perspective. What do they want? What challenges do they face? Reflect on how this changes your understanding of the issue.

3. **Interview a Stakeholder:** Identify one key player in a system you're studying (e.g. a colleague, customer, or community member). Ask them about their priorities and challenges related to the issue. Take notes on what new insights emerge.

Key Takeaway

Systems are shaped by the people and groups within them. Identifying key stakeholders ensures you see the whole picture.

Chapter 3: Trace Causal Links

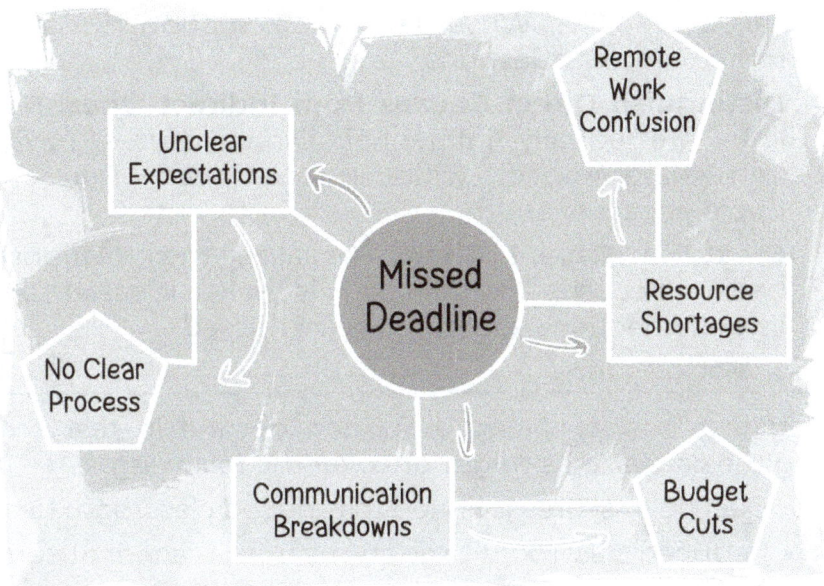

The Chain Reaction of Cause and Effect

Every system behaves the way it does because of an intricate web of consequences. Tracing causal links means following the chain of events and influences to understand why things happen the way they do. It's about moving beyond symptoms and uncovering the forces driving behavior within a system.

Consider a spike in employee turnover at a company. A superficial glance might blame low morale, but tracing the causal links reveals a deeper story: Morale declined because of high workloads, which were caused by understaffing, which stemmed from a budget freeze, which, in turn, resulted from declining profits. Understanding these links allows you to address the root causes instead of just firefighting the symptoms.

How to Trace Causal Links

1. **Start with the Event:** Identify the problem or behavior you want to analyze. Be specific — this is your starting point.

2. **Ask "Why?" Repeatedly:** For each identified cause, ask, "Why is this happening?" Follow the chain until you reach the most fundamental root cause. This is often called the "Five Whys" technique, though it may take more or fewer questions.

3. **Distinguish Direct Causes from Indirect Ones:** Not all links are equally influential. Direct causes have an immediate impact, while indirect ones often create ripple effects over time.

4. **Create a Causal Chart:** Visualize the relationships between causes and effects. This makes it easier to spot interconnections you might have missed.

Real-World Example

Imagine a school facing a sudden decline in test scores. Tracing the causal links might uncover the following:

- Decline in scores is linked to reduced classroom time.
- Reduced classroom time stems from teacher absences.
- Teacher absences are tied to burnout.
- Burnout is linked to increased administrative workloads.

By addressing the root cause — burnout — administrators could significantly improve scores without focusing solely on test preparation.

Why It Matters

Tracing causal links prevents you from wasting time on superficial fixes. It allows you to pinpoint what's truly driving system behavior so you can focus your energy where it matters most. Without this skill, you risk treating symptoms while the underlying issues continue to fester.

Exercises

1. **Causal Chain Analysis:** Pick a recent problem you've encountered. Write it down, then repeatedly ask, "Why is this happening?" until you reach the root cause. Reflect on whether your initial understanding missed anything.

2. **Visualize a Cause Outline:** For a chosen issue, draw a diagram showing all contributing factors and their relationships. Highlight direct causes in one color and indirect ones in another.

3. **Apply in Everyday Life:** The next time you encounter a personal or professional challenge, pause before reacting. Ask yourself, "What caused this situation, and what might have caused that?" Practice tracing causal links to develop this habit.

Key Takeaway

Systems behave the way they do for a reason. Tracing causal links helps you understand why.

Chapter 4: Spot Feedback Loops

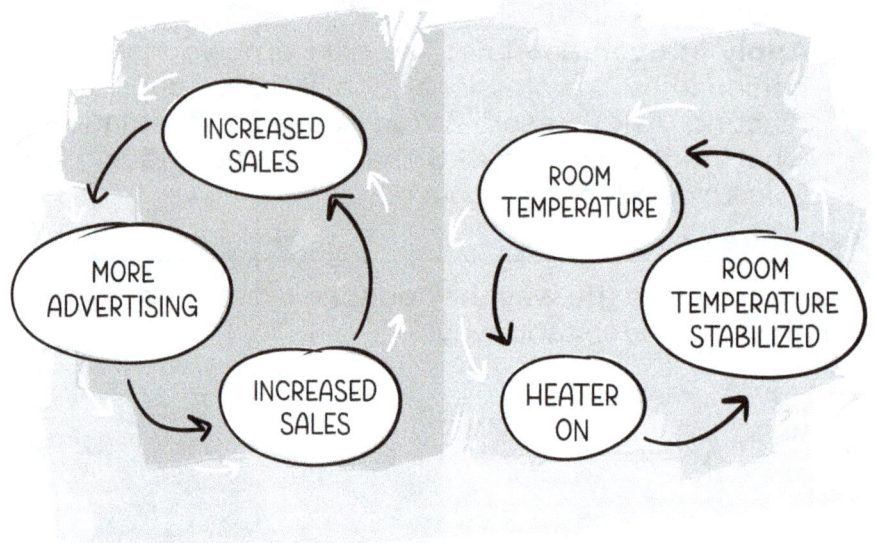

The Cycles That Shape Systems

Feedback loops are the beating heart of any system. They explain why some systems spiral out of control while others stabilize themselves. A feedback loop occurs when a system's output influences its input, creating a cycle. Recognizing these loops is key to understanding system behavior and designing effective interventions.

There are two main types of feedback loops:

1. **Reinforcing Loops** amplify changes. For example, a social media post that gains likes encourages more people to view it, leading to even more likes — a self-reinforcing cycle.

2. **Balancing Loops** counteract changes to maintain stability. For instance, a thermostat balances room temperature by activating heating or cooling as needed.

Spotting recursive patterns in a system lets you anticipate behaviors, whether it's exponential growth, collapse, or equilibrium.

How to Spot Feedback Loops

1. **Look for Recurring Cycles:** Identify situations where outputs loop back into the system to influence future behavior.

2. **Chart the Flow:** Diagram the relationships between elements, showing how one affects another. Pay attention to where the process forms a closed loop.

3. **Distinguish Between Reinforcing and Balancing Loops:**
   - Reinforcing loops escalate or amplify changes.
   - Balancing loops regulate or stabilize the system.

4. **Identify Delays:** Many feedback loops involve time lags, where the effects of an action aren't immediately visible. Recognizing these delays helps predict outcomes more accurately.

Real-World Example

Take urban traffic congestion. A reinforcing feedback loop occurs when increased car use leads to longer commute times, prompting even more people to rely on cars instead of public transport. A balancing loop could involve toll charges that discourage excessive driving, stabilizing traffic levels. Recognizing these loops allows city planners to design interventions that break harmful cycles and strengthen stabilizing ones.

Why It Matters

Feedback loops are the underlying drivers of many systemic behaviors. Without recognizing them, you may misinterpret patterns, waste effort addressing symptoms, or unintentionally make problems worse. Understanding these loops allows you to predict outcomes and intervene effectively.

Exercises

1. **Feedback Mapping:** Choose a recurring issue you've observed (e.g. productivity cycles at work, mood swings, or resource shortages). Create a simple diagram showing the feedback loop that drives it.

2. **Identify Reinforcing vs. Balancing Loops:** Look at a system you interact with daily (e.g. a budgeting process or exercise routine) and identify whether the cycles involved are reinforcing or balancing.

3. **Test for Delays:** Reflect on a situation where you noticed delayed consequences (e.g. implementing a new policy or adopting a new habit). Lay out how the delay affected the feedback loop.

Key Takeaway:

Feedback loops are the engines of system behavior — spotting them lets you predict and shape outcomes.

Chapter 5: Unpack Delay Dynamics

The Waiting Game of Systems

Delays are the hidden time bombs in every system. They occur when there's a gap between cause and effect, often making it difficult to see how actions influence outcomes. This can lead to impatience, poor decisions, or unintended consequences.

For example, consider starting a new workout routine. You won't see results immediately; the benefits come after weeks of consistent effort. Without understanding this delay, you might assume the routine isn't working and give up prematurely. Similarly, in larger systems, ignoring delays can lead to overcorrections or destabilization.

How to Recognize Delays

1. **Identify Where Action Meets Response:** Look for areas where the system takes time to react. These could be physical delays (e.g. shipping times), human delays (e.g.

decision-making processes), or environmental delays (e.g. climate response to emissions).

2. **Separate Immediate from Long-Term Effects:** Distinguish between outcomes that occur right away and those that emerge later.

3. **Analyze the Gap:** Estimate the time lag between action and result. This helps you predict when effects will appear and avoid overreacting in the meantime.

4. **Account for Compounding Effects:** Recognize how delays can amplify or obscure the system's behavior over time.

Real-World Example

In agriculture, overusing fertilizer might initially boost crop yields, leading farmers to assume the strategy is working. However, the delayed effect of soil degradation could cause long-term productivity losses. Recognizing these dynamics allows for sustainable practices that balance short-term gains with long-term health.

Why It Matters

Delays make systems tricky to manage. Reacting too soon may cause overcorrections, while acting too late risks irreversible damage. By understanding delay dynamics, you can better predict outcomes, avoid hasty decisions, and design strategies that account for the system's natural pace.

Exercises

1. **Identify a Delay:** Think of a situation where you experienced a delay between action and result (e.g. a project rollout or personal habit change). Write down the immediate and delayed effects and reflect on how the delay influenced your response.

2. **Analyze a System with Delays:** Choose a system (e.g. a supply chain, education process, or health goal). Pinpoint where delays occur and how they affect the system's overall behavior.

3. **Set a Patience Strategy:** For a goal you're currently working toward, list potential delays you might encounter and plan how to stay consistent during the waiting period.

Key Takeaway

Delays obscure cause-and-effect relationships. Understanding them helps you predict and manage outcomes effectively.

Chapter 6: Look for System Boundaries

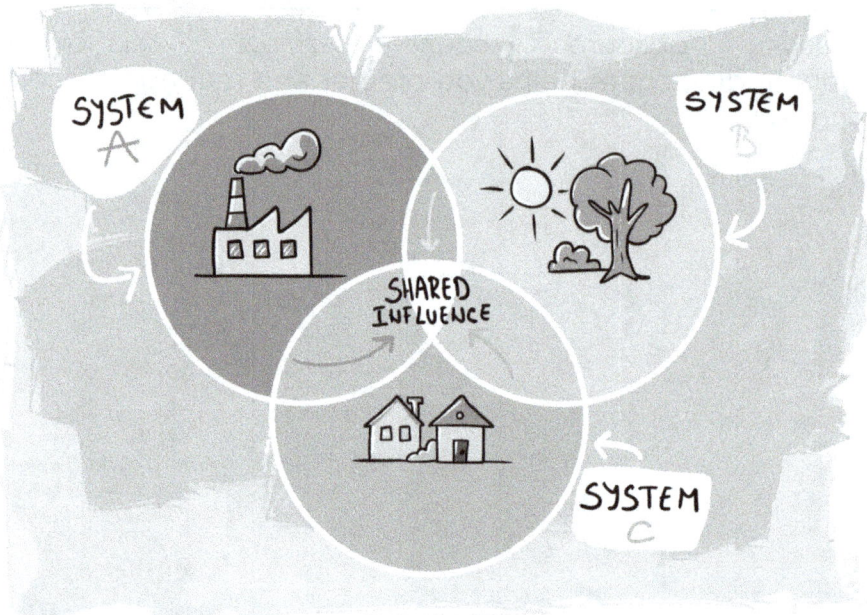

Defining the Edges of a System

Systems can also be defined as ecosystems — they operate within boundaries that define what is part of the system and what lies outside it. But unlike physical fences, these boundaries are often conceptual and shaped by the observer's perspective. The boundaries you choose to define will impact how you understand a system and the solutions you propose.

Systems can also overlap. For instance: A public school system intersects with community organizations, local businesses, and even state policies. If you ignore these overlaps, you might overlook critical influences that shape the system's behavior.

How to Identify System Boundaries

1. **Define What's In and Out:** Start by listing the elements you think belong to the system. Then, list what might lie outside of it but still interact with it. For example, in a company, the core system might include employees, managers, and tools, while external elements like suppliers and customers interact with it.

2. **Look for Overlaps:** Most systems don't operate in isolation. Think about where your system might intersect with others. For instance, a healthcare system overlaps with public transportation when patients need to reach hospitals.

3. **Acknowledge Flexibility:** Remember that boundaries are often artificial. For example, a marketing campaign might seem internal to a business, but it extends into the customer's world, influencing their behavior. Boundaries should evolve as your understanding of the system deepens.

4. **Watch for Boundary Changes:** Systems are dynamic, and their boundaries can shift over time. A small start-up might initially include only a handful of employees but later expand to contractors, suppliers, and global teams.

Real-World Example

Take climate change as an example. Initially, people viewed it as a system limited to environmental science. But over time, we've expanded the boundary to include energy policies, economic systems, and even social behaviors. Ignoring these broader boundaries would lead to ineffective solutions, such as addressing emissions from power plants but overlooking consumer behavior or global trade policies.

Why It Matters

Where you draw the line around a system shapes your understanding of it. If your boundary is too narrow, you may overlook critical influences or connections. If it's too broad, you risk becoming overwhelmed by irrelevant details. The key is to define boundaries that help you focus on what's important while staying aware of external forces.

Exercises

1. **Boundary Layout:** Think of a system you interact with daily, like your household budget. Write down what you include as part of the system (income, expenses, savings) and what you exclude. Then ask: Are there external factors (e.g. market trends) that influence it? Reflect on how adjusting the boundary changes your understanding.

2. **Analyze Overlapping Systems:** Pick two systems that interact in your life, such as your workplace and your family life. Create a diagram that shows where their boundaries overlap and how that interaction affects your decisions.

3. **Reassess a System Boundary:** Look at a problem you've analyzed before. Redraw the system's boundaries to include elements you initially excluded. What new insights or opportunities emerge?

Key Takeaway

Understanding and adjusting system boundaries lets you see the system more clearly, ensuring you include all relevant factors while avoiding unnecessary complexity.

Chapter 7: Observe Resource Flows

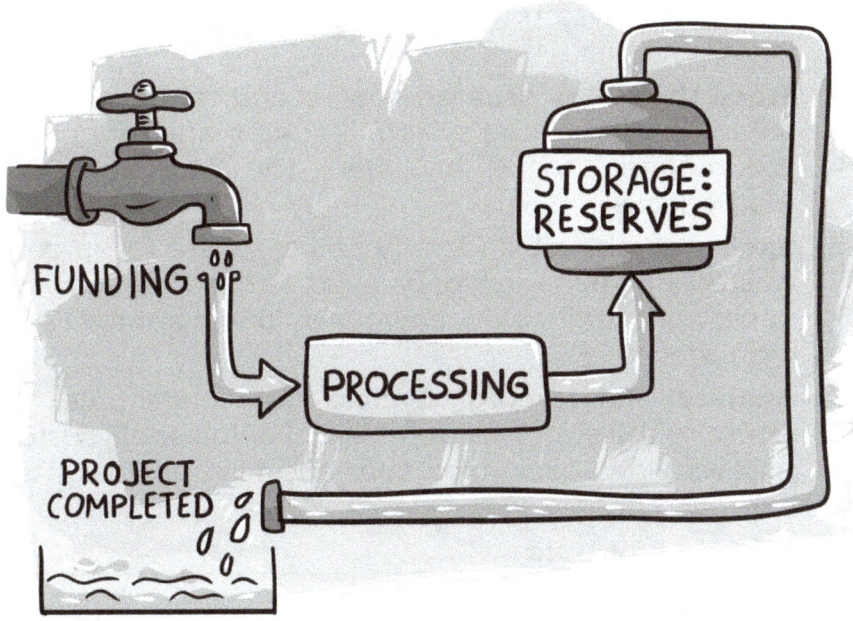

Follow the Flow

Every system relies on the movement of resources. These could be tangible resources, such as water or materials, or intangible ones, like knowledge or influence. Observing resource flows helps you understand how the system sustains itself, identifies inefficiencies, and reveals points of accumulation or loss.

Consider a supply chain. Resources like raw materials flow from suppliers to manufacturers, then to distributors, and finally to customers. At each stage, there may be delays, bottlenecks, or losses. By observing the flow of these resources, businesses can pinpoint inefficiencies, reduce waste, and improve performance.

Resource flows also exist in non-physical systems. For instance, in a workplace, knowledge flows from leadership to employees, while feedback flows in the opposite direction.

Understanding these flows can improve communication and decision-making.

How to Observe Resource Flows

1. **Identify Inputs and Outputs:** Start by listing what enters the system (e.g. money, energy, or ideas) and what leaves it.

2. **Trace the Path:** Visualize how resources move between different parts of the system. Look for areas where they accumulate (stocks) or where the flow slows down (bottlenecks).

3. **Spot Inefficiencies:** Identify points where resources are wasted, mismanaged, or delayed. For example, excessive paperwork might slow down the flow of approvals in an organization.

4. **Analyze Reinforcing Cycles:** Some resource flows return to the system as feedback. For instance, customer reviews flow back into the business as insights for improvement.

Real-World Example

Think about energy use in a household. Electricity flows into the home, powering appliances and lighting. Along the way, inefficiencies like poor insulation or outdated devices cause energy loss. Observing this flow allows homeowners to make targeted improvements, like installing energy-efficient windows or upgrading appliances, to reduce waste and costs.

Why It Matters

Resource flows are the lifeblood of a system. Mismanaging them leads to inefficiencies, shortages, or even system failure. By understanding these flows, you can identify opportunities to improve performance, reduce waste, and make the system more sustainable.

Exercises

1. **Track a Resource:** Choose a resource you use daily (e.g. water, time, or money). Map its flow from input to output, noting where it accumulates or is wasted.

2. **Flow Diagram:** Pick a system you interact with, like your office workflow. Create a diagram showing the flow of information or tasks and highlight where delays or bottlenecks occur.

3. **Improve a Flow:** Identify a flow you want to optimize — like your daily schedule. Look for points where time or energy is wasted and brainstorm ways to streamline the process.

Key Takeaway

Understanding how resources flow through a system helps you spot inefficiencies, optimize performance, and ensure sustainability.

Chapter 8: Notice Points of Tension

The Push and Pull of Systems

Systems are rarely in perfect harmony. Instead, they are shaped by competing forces pulling in different directions. These points of tension often highlight areas of instability or inefficiency within the system. Recognizing them allows you to diagnose challenges, resolve conflicts, and design solutions that balance competing priorities.

For example, a company might face tension between its need for innovation (which requires risk-taking) and its need for stability (which requires adherence to proven processes). If this tension goes unmanaged, it could lead to burnout, conflict, or stagnation. However, by identifying and addressing the tension, the company can find ways to encourage innovation without sacrificing stability.

How to Identify Points of Tension

1. **Look for Symptoms:** Tensions often manifest as recurring problems, such as delays, conflicts, or inefficiencies. Ask yourself what forces might be pulling against each other.

2. **Identify Trade-Offs:** Consider where the system forces you to choose between competing goals, such as speed vs. accuracy or cost vs. quality.

3. **Pinpoint Hotspots:** Focus on areas where these tensions are most visible, such as team disagreements, overused resources, or missed deadlines.

4. **Ask Why the Tension Exists:** Trace the root causes of the tension. For example, is it due to external pressures, conflicting priorities, or misaligned incentives?

Real-World Example

Consider a non-profit organization working to expand its reach. The tension lies between fundraising efforts (to support growth) and program delivery (to meet current needs). Ignoring this tension could stretch resources too thin, compromising both goals. Recognizing the tension allows the organization to strategically allocate resources, balancing immediate impact with future sustainability.

Why It Matters

Points of tension reveal where systems are under stress. Ignoring these areas risks escalation and failure, while addressing them creates opportunities for growth, resolution, and balance.

Exercises

1. **Tension Diagram:** Identify a system in your life with recurring challenges (e.g. work-life balance). List the forces pulling in opposite directions and reflect on how they influence each other.

2. **Visualize a Trade-Off:** Draw a simple chart with two competing priorities (e.g. cost vs. quality). Plot current and desired states to see where adjustments are needed.

3. **Explore Root Causes:** Pick a recurring tension in your workplace or personal life. Ask why it exists and what changes could ease the strain.

Key Takeaway

Tensions highlight the competing forces shaping a system. Addressing them leads to better balance and long-term success.

Chapter 9: Uncover Emergent Behavior

The Power of Emergence

Some of the most fascinating aspects of systems are behaviors that arise spontaneously from interactions between parts. These are called emergent behaviors. Unlike predictable outputs of simple systems, emergent behaviors are often surprising and cannot be easily traced to a single cause. They occur when individual components of a system interact in ways that produce something greater than the sum of its parts.

Consider a traffic system. The collective movement of traffic jams emerges not from individual drivers but from how their decisions interact — accelerating, braking, merging — all within the broader constraints of road design and traffic laws. Similarly, in nature, a beehive's intricate organization emerges from the actions of individual bees following simple rules.

Emergent behavior can be constructive or destructive. In business, for instance, creativity can emerge from collaboration, while chaos might emerge from poor communication. Understanding how and why emergence occurs allows you to harness it for positive outcomes and mitigate its downsides.

How to Recognize Emergent Behavior

1. **Look Beyond Individual Actions:** Focus on how the collective behavior of a system differs from the behavior of its parts. For example, a single employee working overtime won't affect much, but a culture of overwork across an organization could lead to widespread burnout.

2. **Identify Simple Rules or Interactions:** Emergence often stems from simple behaviors. In an ant colony, ants don't "plan" their foraging routes; they leave pheromone trails that others follow, creating complex, efficient networks.

3. **Analyze Unexpected Outcomes:** If the system produces outcomes that can't be explained by its individual components, emergence is likely at play.

4. **Trace Recursive Patterns:** Emergent behaviors often reinforce themselves through dynamic interconnections. For example, viral trends on social media arise when user interactions (likes, shares, comments) amplify visibility, creating a self-reinforcing cycle.

Real-World Example

In financial markets, stock prices are influenced by countless individual investors making decisions based on available information. The emergent behavior of the market — such as bubbles or crashes — results not from any single investor but from how their actions collectively interact within the system. Recognizing this can help analysts predict and prepare for these large-scale events.

Why It Matters

Emergent behaviors are often unpredictable and can either be a system's greatest strength or its Achilles' heel. Failing to account for emergence can lead to surprises, such as unintended consequences of policies or plans. However, when understood, emergence can be used to foster creativity, innovation, and resilience within a system.

Exercises

1. **Observe Emergence in Nature:** Spend time observing natural systems like bird flocks, schools of fish, or ant colonies. Reflect on how their behaviors result from interactions rather than centralized control.

2. **Analyze a Group Dynamic:** Think about a group you belong to (e.g. your workplace or a community). Identify behaviors or outcomes that emerge from the group's interactions, such as shared values or recurring conflicts.

3. **Harness Positive Emergence:** Choose a project or team you're part of and brainstorm ways to encourage interactions that lead to constructive outcomes, like fostering collaboration or open communication.

Key Takeaway

Emergent behavior arises from interactions between parts of a system — understanding it helps you harness its potential and anticipate its challenges.

Chapter 10: Understand System History

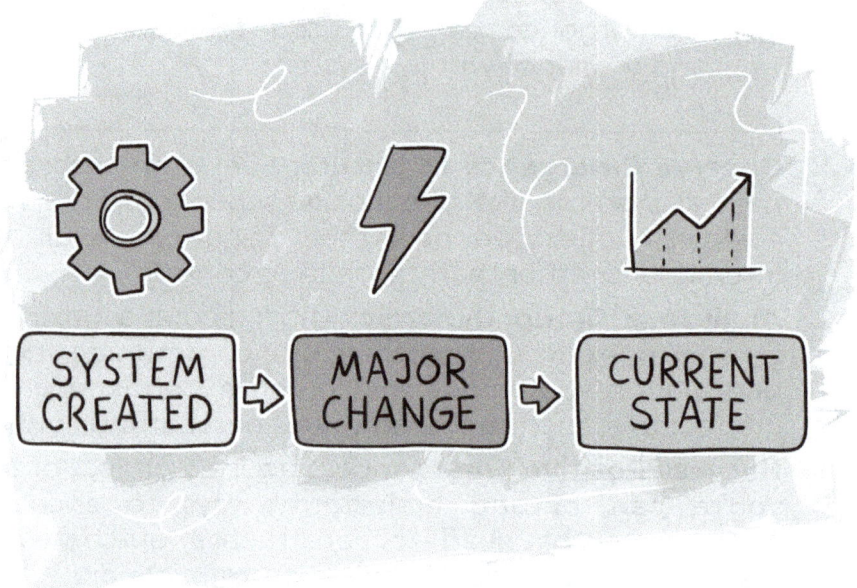

SYSTEM CREATED ⇨ **MAJOR CHANGE** ⇨ **CURRENT STATE**

Every System Has a Story

To understand why a system behaves the way it does today, you need to look at where it came from. Systems are shaped by their histories, with past decisions, events, and interactions creating the conditions you see now. Whether it's a company's organizational structure, a city's infrastructure, or a natural ecosystem, its history holds the clues to understanding its present and shaping its future.

For example, consider a company struggling with low employee morale. A superficial analysis might point to current leadership. But digging into the company's history might reveal a deeper story: years of layoffs, missed opportunities for innovation, and a legacy of poor communication. These historical factors contribute to the current state and provide insight into how to address the root issues.

1. **Trace the Origin:** Start by asking, "Where did this system come from?" Identify its purpose at creation and how it has evolved.

2. **Identify Key Events:** Look for major turning points, such as leadership changes, policy shifts, or external disruptions. These events often create lasting impacts.

3. **Follow the Chain of Decisions:** Systems are shaped by decisions over time. Understanding the rationale behind these decisions — whether good or bad — helps you identify where the system succeeded or went off track.

4. **Assess Path Dependencies:** Many systems become "locked in" by past choices, making certain paths easier to follow and others harder. For example, a city built around cars may struggle to pivot to public transportation due to existing infrastructure investments.

Real-World Example

Consider the U.S. healthcare system. Its complexity and challenges are deeply rooted in historical events, such as the employer-based insurance model introduced during World War II, the introduction of Medicare and Medicaid in the 1960s, and subsequent policy changes. Without understanding this history, reform efforts often miss the systemic constraints and opportunities for meaningful change.

Why It Matters

Understanding a system's history prevents you from making superficial judgments or misdiagnosing problems. It also helps you avoid repeating past mistakes. By seeing how the present has been shaped by the past, you can make more informed decisions about the future.

Exercises

1. **Create a System Timeline:** Choose a system you're part of (e.g. your workplace or community) and define its key events. Reflect on how these events shaped the current state.

2. **Analyze Path Dependencies:** Identify a decision in your life or work that's been constrained by past choices (e.g. choosing a tool because it's already in use). Reflect on whether these constraints are still valid.

3. **Ask "What if?":** Imagine how the system might look today if a key event in its history had unfolded differently. Consider what lessons this alternate history might offer for the future.

Key Takeaway

A system's present behavior is rooted in its past. Understanding its history gives you the insights to shape its future.

Chapter 11: Visualize Interconnections

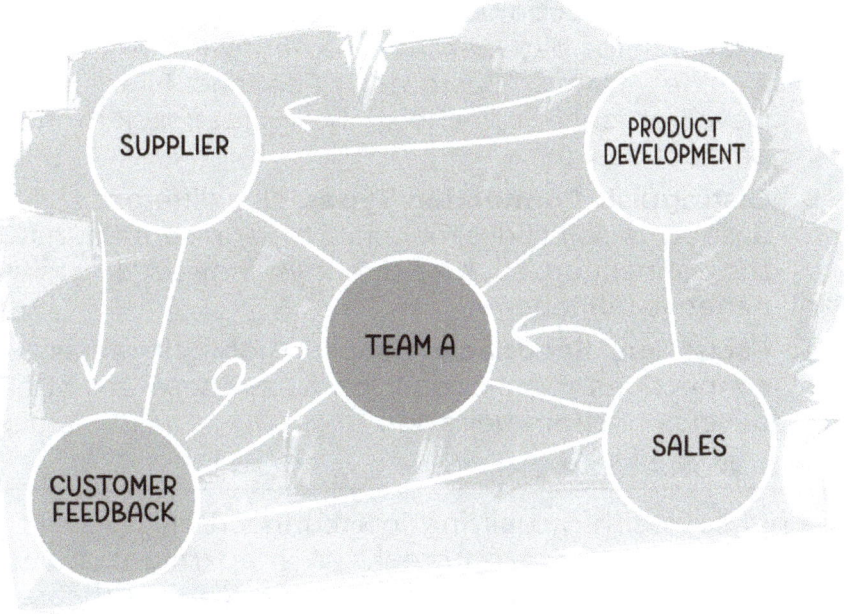

The Power of Seeing Connections

Systems are made up of interconnected parts, and those connections often determine how the system behaves. Visualizing interconnections allows you to understand the relationships between components and understand the flow of influence. Without this visualization, connections may remain invisible, leaving you unaware of key dynamics.

For example, imagine a small business facing declining sales. A surface-level analysis might focus on marketing strategies. But a visual guide could reveal connections to other factors, such as product quality, supply chain delays, or customer service issues. Seeing the entire web of influences enables a more holistic understanding of the problem.

How to Visualize Interconnections

1. **Identify the Key Elements:** Start by listing all the major parts of the system. This could include people, processes, resources, or external influences.

2. **Draw Connections:** Use arrows or lines to indicate relationships between the elements. For example, draw a line from "Customer Feedback" to "Product Development" to show how feedback influences product design.

3. **Distinguish Connection Types:** Use different styles (e.g. dashed vs. solid lines) or colors to represent the nature of the connection, such as direct vs. indirect or positive vs. negative influence.

4. **Focus on Feedback Loops:** Highlight areas where connections form closed loops, as these are often the drivers of system behavior.

Real-World Example

In public health, visualizing interconnections is essential for understanding disease outbreaks. A map might show how factors like population density, access to healthcare, and vaccination rates interact. This helps policymakers see the big picture, identify weak points in the system, and design targeted interventions.

Why It Matters

When you visualize interconnections, you make the system's complexity visible. This prevents you from focusing too narrowly on individual components and instead encourages you to see how the whole system operates. Understanding these relationships helps you identify leverage points, anticipate ripple effects, and design more effective solutions.

Exercises

1. **Create a System Structure:** Choose a system you interact with (e.g. your workplace or community) and list its key components. Draw a diagram showing how they influence one another, using arrows to represent connections.

2. **Focus on One Connection:** Pick a single connection from your map (e.g. between two teams or departments). Analyze how strengthening or weakening this connection might affect the system.

3. **Look for Overlooked Links:** Review your plan and ask, "Are there any connections I missed?" Add these and reflect on how they change your understanding of the system.

Key Takeaway

Visualizing interconnections helps you understand how the parts of a system interact, revealing opportunities to improve its behavior.

Chapter 12: Distinguish Stocks from Flows

The Building Blocks of Systems

To truly understand how systems function, you need to grasp the distinction between stocks and flows. Stocks are accumulations within a system — resources, people, energy, or information that build up over time. Flows, on the other hand, are the movement of those resources into or out of the system.

Consider a savings account. The account balance is a stock, while deposits and withdrawals are flows. The balance only changes when the inflow (deposits) exceeds the outflow (withdrawals), or vice versa. Understanding these dynamics is key to managing systems effectively.

How to Distinguish Stocks from Flows

1. **Identify What's Being Accumulated:** Look for quantities that build up over time, such as money, energy, or people. These are the stocks.

2. **Trace Inflows and Outflows:** Determine what adds to or depletes the stock. For example, a population's stock grows through births (inflows) and shrinks through deaths and migration (outflows).

3. **Consider Time Lags:** Stocks often act as buffers, absorbing changes in inflows and outflows. Recognizing these delays helps you predict how the system will respond to interventions.

4. **Visualize the Relationship:** Use a diagram to define the stocks and flows in the system. This makes it easier to see how changes in flows affect the stock over time.

Real-World Example

In environmental systems, forests act as a stock of carbon, storing CO_2 over decades. The flows include carbon absorption (via tree growth) and carbon release (via deforestation or wildfires). Policies aimed at reducing atmospheric CO_2 must address both inflows and outflows to manage this stock effectively.

Why It Matters

Confusing stocks and flows leads to poor decision-making. For example, in managing budgets, focusing only on monthly income (a flow) while ignoring savings (a stock) could result in financial instability. By distinguishing between the two, you gain clarity on how systems accumulate, deplete, and stabilize over time.

Exercises

1. **Analyze a Stock and Flow:** Choose a system in your life (e.g. household expenses). Identify one stock (e.g. your savings) and its inflows (income) and outflows (expenses). Reflect on how changing the flows would affect the stock.

2. **Track a Stock Over Time:** Pick a stock (e.g. your energy levels) and observe how it changes throughout the day. Identify the inflows (rest, food) and outflows (work, exercise) affecting it.

3. **Create a Stock-Flow Diagram:** Choose a system, such as a water supply or project timeline. Use a simple diagram to illustrate its stocks and flows, noting how they influence one another.

Key Takeaway

Distinguishing stocks from flows helps you understand how resources accumulate, deplete, and stabilize within a system.

Chapter 13: Notice Self-Organization

The Magic of Systems That Organize Themselves

Not all systems require a leader to function effectively. Some systems have the remarkable ability to organize themselves without external control. This phenomenon, called self-organization, occurs when the components of a system interact in ways that lead to structure, order, or patterns — often spontaneously.

Consider a flock of birds flying in perfect unison. There's no single leader directing their movements; instead, each bird follows simple rules, such as maintaining a certain distance and mirroring the direction of its neighbors. Together, their interactions create the stunning, cohesive behavior that can often be seen.

Self-organization isn't limited to nature. Social systems, markets, and even certain technologies exhibit self-organizing behavior. Recognizing this phenomenon allows you to understand how systems adapt, evolve, and maintain stability on their own—and how you can work with, rather than against, this natural order.

How to Recognize Self-Organization

1. **Look for Patterns Without Central Control:** Identify systems where order emerges from individual actions rather than top-down planning. For example, in a marketplace, prices adjust dynamically based on the actions of buyers and sellers, not a central authority.

2. **Find the Simple Rules:** Self-organization often arises from simple, localized interactions. In an ant colony, ants leave pheromone trails that others follow, collectively creating efficient foraging paths.

3. **Observe Adaptation:** Self-organizing systems can adjust to changes in their environment. For example, ecosystems adapt to disturbances by reorganizing themselves around available resources.

4. **Spot Decentralized Feedback Loops:** These systems rely on feedback from their components to maintain order. For instance, traffic flow adjusts as individual drivers respond to road conditions, creating an overall pattern.

Real-World Example

Online platforms often exhibit self-organization. Consider Wikipedia: its articles are created, edited, and refined by individual contributors following a few simple rules, such as providing citations and adhering to neutral language. The result is a comprehensive and dynamic knowledge base with no single editor in charge.

Why It Matters

Understanding self-organization helps you see that not all systems require micromanagement. Intervening too heavily in a self-organizing system can disrupt its natural balance. For example, imposing rigid rules on a creative team might stifle the organic collaboration that leads to innovation. By recognizing and respecting self-organization, you can design systems that foster resilience, adaptability, and creativity.

Exercises

1. **Observe a Self-Organizing System:** Spend time watching a system that organizes itself, such as a group of people queuing in a crowded space or a school of fish swimming together. Reflect on what simple rules or interactions drive the system's order.

2. **Analyze Your Workplace:** Identify areas where your team or organization exhibits self-organization. What rules allow this to happen? How can you support these natural dynamics?

3. **Design for Self-Organization:** Choose a project or task and create conditions that allow the system to organize itself. For example, instead of assigning tasks directly, provide general goals and let the team decide how to achieve them.

Key Takeaway

Self-organizing systems create structure and order without external control. Understanding this dynamic allows you to design systems that harness natural adaptability and creativity.

Chapter 14: Focus on Tipping Points

When Small Changes Create Big Shifts

Every system has thresholds — moments when a small change can cause a dramatic shift. These are called tipping points. At these critical moments, a system transitions from one state to another, often irreversibly.

Think of a snow-covered mountainside. For hours, snow piles up harmlessly. Then, one final snowflake lands, and an avalanche is triggered. It wasn't the size of the snowflake that mattered, but the fact that the system had reached its tipping point.

Tipping points can lead to both positive and negative outcomes. In social movements, a single event can galvanize mass participation, transforming the movement overnight. In environmental systems, crossing a tipping point might result in irreversible damage, such as the melting of polar ice caps.

Recognizing tipping points helps you anticipate change and identify where small actions can have the greatest impact.

How to Identify Tipping Points

1. **Understand System Thresholds:** Identify the conditions under which the system might shift states. For example, in a workplace, morale may reach a tipping point where even one more unresolved issue triggers widespread dissatisfaction.

2. **Track Early Warning Signs:** Tipping points are often preceded by small, incremental changes. For instance, a rising temperature in a server room might lead to sudden system failure once a critical heat threshold is crossed.

3. **Recognize Nonlinear Behavior:** In many systems, change is not gradual — it accelerates suddenly as the tipping point approaches. Monitor patterns for signs of such rapid escalation.

4. **Focus on Leverage Points:** Tipping points are often influenced by specific areas of the system where small interventions can create outsized effects.

Real-World Example

In public health, tipping points play a key role in epidemic outbreaks. Initially, a few isolated cases of a disease may seem manageable. But once the infection rate crosses a critical threshold, the disease can spread exponentially, overwhelming healthcare systems. Identifying and addressing this tipping point early — through measures such as vaccination campaigns — can prevent catastrophe.

Why It Matters

Tipping points represent moments of opportunity and risk. If you act too late, you may face consequences that are difficult or impossible to reverse. But if you recognize a tipping point early, you can take targeted actions to steer the system in a desired direction.

Exercises

1. **Reflect on Personal Tipping Points:** Think of a time in your life when a small decision or event caused a major change (e.g. choosing a career path or joining a new social group). What conditions made that tipping point possible?

2. **Analyze a System at Risk:** Choose a system you're part of and identify any thresholds it may be approaching (e.g. team burnout or financial instability). What small actions could prevent a negative tipping point or encourage a positive one?

3. **Create a Tipping Point Strategy:** For a goal you're working toward, identify the leverage points where small efforts could create significant progress. Plan how to focus your energy on these critical areas.

Key Takeaway

Tipping points are moments when small changes create big shifts — understanding them allows you to anticipate risks and seize opportunities.

Chapter 15: See Patterns Across Scales

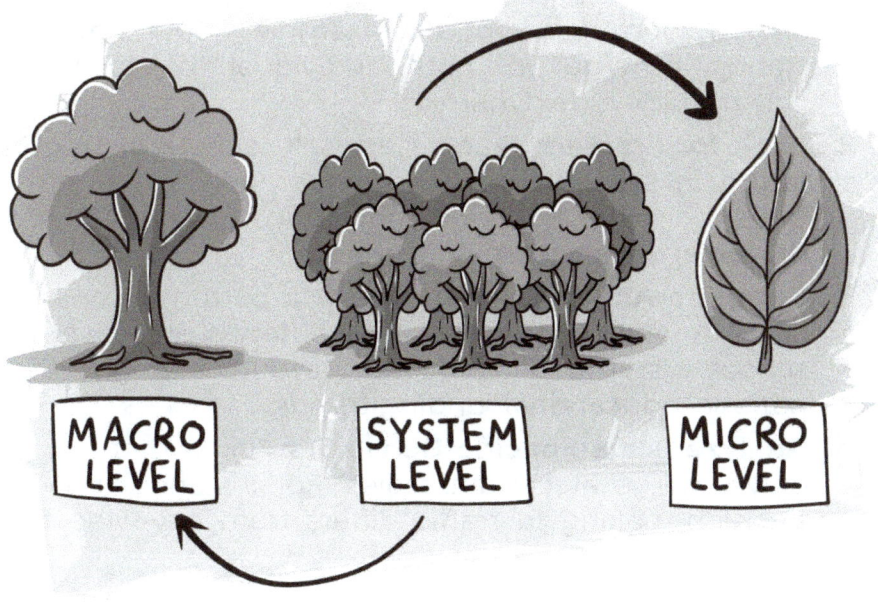

MACRO LEVEL   SYSTEM LEVEL   MICRO LEVEL

Patterns at Every Level

Systems often exhibit patterns that repeat across different scales. This concept, called scale invariance, is key to understanding how systems behave in both the smallest details and the biggest structures. By recognizing patterns across scales, you gain insight into how small actions influence larger systems — and vice versa.

For example, in a business, the communication patterns within a small team may mirror those of the entire organization. A team prone to silos might reflect a larger organizational culture of fragmented departments. Conversely, changes at the macro scale — such as company-wide policy shifts — often trickle down and reshape the micro scale.

The ability to see patterns across scales is like having a zoom lens for systems. It allows you to connect the dots between what happens at different levels, making your understanding of the system far more robust.

How to Spot Patterns Across Scales

1. **Zoom In and Out:** Start at one level — micro, macro, or in between — and observe how patterns repeat or shift as you zoom in or out. For example, notice how social trends emerge in both individual behaviors and community-wide dynamics.

2. **Look for Fractals:** Fractals are self-repeating structures found in systems, such as the branching patterns of trees or river networks. Spotting these can reveal universal rules governing the system.

3. **Compare Across Levels:** Identify a pattern at one scale and ask whether it exists at other levels. For example, a school system's allocation of resources might mirror national educational funding trends.

4. **Analyze Scale-Specific Behaviors:** Some patterns may only emerge at certain scales. For instance, individual decision-making in traffic differs from city-wide traffic flow patterns.

Real-World Example

Climate systems offer a striking example of patterns across scales. At the smallest scale, changes in plant respiration influence local carbon dioxide levels. Zooming out, these changes aggregate to affect regional weather patterns, which in turn influence global climate. Recognizing this interconnectedness helps scientists predict and address climate change at all levels.

Why It Matters

Failing to see patterns across scales can lead to blind spots. A solution that works at the micro level may not address larger issues, while focusing solely on the macro level risks missing key details. By analyzing multiple scales, you can design solutions that are effective and aligned with the system's dynamics as a whole.

Exercises

1. **Zoom In and Out on a System:** Pick a system you're familiar with, such as your workplace. Observe how patterns at the team level reflect or differ from those at the organizational level. Write down your observations.

2. **Identify Fractals in Nature or Life:** Spend time observing systems like trees, rivers, or family structures. Look for self-repeating patterns that appear across different scales. Reflect on what these patterns reveal about the system.

3. **Compare Solutions Across Scales:** Think about a recent problem you solved (e.g. improving your daily schedule). Consider how that solution might work at a larger scale (e.g. managing a team) or smaller scale (e.g. personal habits).

Key Takeaway

Recognizing patterns across scales helps you understand how systems behave at every level, from the micro to the macro.

Chapter 16: Look for Missing Connections

The Power of What's Missing

When analyzing a system, it's tempting to focus solely on what's present: the visible people, processes, and interactions driving its behavior. However, just as important are the connections that *should* exist but don't. Missing connections act like broken links in a chain, interrupting the flow of resources, information, or influence, and leaving the system vulnerable to inefficiencies, delays, or even collapse.

Consider a workplace where departments operate in silos. Each team focuses on its tasks without communicating with others. The absence of collaboration means missed opportunities to share insights, align goals, or avoid redundant efforts. Similarly, in urban planning, a lack of coordination between transportation and housing developers can lead to neighborhoods poorly served by public transit.

Identifying these gaps is like finding the missing pieces of a puzzle. Once they are acknowledged and addressed, the system becomes more cohesive and efficient.

How to Identify Missing Connections

1. **Outline the System:** Start by sketching out the system's components and the connections between them. Focus on how resources, information, or influence flow from one part to another.

2. **Spot the Breaks:** Look for interruptions in the flow—places where resources should move seamlessly but don't. For instance, is a lack of communication between teams causing project delays?

3. **Ask "What's Missing?":** Step back and ask whether new connections could improve the system. For example, would connecting two previously isolated departments foster collaboration?

4. **Test New Connections:** Experiment with bridging the gaps. Introduce a feedback mechanism or communication channel between disconnected components and observe how it changes the system's behavior.

Real-World Example

Consider healthcare systems, where missing connections often lead to inefficiencies. A patient might visit multiple specialists, but without a shared medical record, doctors lack access to the full picture of the patient's condition. This gap increases the risk of misdiagnosis or redundant tests. Implementing electronic health records bridges this connection, enabling doctors, pharmacists, and patients to collaborate effectively.

Why It Matters

Missing connections create inefficiencies, waste, and vulnerabilities within a system. Ignoring these gaps can perpetuate problems or even cause systemic failures. Conversely, identifying and addressing them unlocks opportunities for improvement, creating stronger and more efficient systems.

For instance, adding a simple communication channel between two teams can transform how they collaborate. Similarly, connecting isolated parts of a supply chain can streamline operations, reduce costs, and improve customer satisfaction.

Exercises

1. **Identify Missing Links:** Choose a system you interact with regularly, such as a workplace process or community project. Sketch its components and connections. Highlight areas where connections are missing and reflect on how those gaps affect the system.

2. **Spot a Missed Opportunity:** Think of a situation where poor communication or coordination caused a problem. Identify which connection was missing and how bridging it might have changed the outcome.

3. **Create a New Connection:** In your personal or professional life, find a missing connection (e.g. between two colleagues or departments). Introduce a way to link them, such as regular meetings or a shared tool, and observe how the system improves.

Key Takeaway

Missing connections weaken systems by disrupting the flow of resources or information — bridging these gaps strengthens the system and creates new opportunities for efficiency.

Chapter 17: Assess System Resilience

Strength in the Face of Challenges

Resilience is the ability of a system to withstand shocks, recover from disruptions, and continue functioning. It's a defining characteristic of systems that survive and thrive over time. In a resilient system, stressors may cause temporary setbacks, but the system adapts and stabilizes without breaking.

Imagine a resilient community facing a natural disaster. Strong emergency services, clear communication, and well-coordinated recovery efforts allow the community to bounce back quickly. In contrast, a community lacking these features might take years to recover — or never fully regain stability. The difference lies in the system's ability to absorb challenges and adapt to new conditions.

Assessing resilience allows you to pinpoint strengths, vulnerabilities, and areas where the system might fail under pressure. This understanding helps you build systems that are better equipped to handle change and disruption.

How to Unpack System Resilience

1. **Identify Vulnerabilities:** Look for areas where the system is most likely to break down under stress. For example, does a workplace rely too heavily on one key employee?

2. **Evaluate Redundancies:** Resilient systems often have backups or alternative pathways. For instance, a resilient transportation system includes multiple modes of travel, such as buses, trains, and bike lanes.

3. **Assess Flexibility:** Resilient systems can adapt to new conditions. For example, a company that quickly shifts to remote work during a crisis demonstrates flexibility.

4. **Test Recovery Capacity:** Consider how well the system can recover after a disruption. Does it bounce back quickly, or does it take too long to regain stability?

Real-World Example

The COVID-19 pandemic revealed stark differences in resilience across industries. Companies with strong digital infrastructures and flexible work policies adapted quickly to remote work, maintaining productivity. In contrast, businesses without these features faced significant disruptions. Assessing and improving resilience in advance could have minimized these impacts.

Why It Matters

Without resilience, systems are fragile and prone to collapse under pressure. A resilient system, however, can endure shocks, adapt to change, and emerge stronger. For example, a resilient organization with cross-trained employees can maintain operations even if key staff are unavailable. Similarly, a resilient personal schedule with built-in flexibility allows you to adapt to unexpected events without stress.

Strengthening resilience isn't just about preparing for worst-case scenarios; it's about building systems that thrive in uncertain and dynamic environments.

Exercises

1. **Reflect on a Past Disruption:** Think of a time when a system you relied on faced a disruption (e.g. a delayed project or personal setback). What made the system resilient — or why did it struggle to recover?

2. **Analyze Redundancies:** Choose a system in your life, such as a financial plan or a team workflow. Identify areas where you have backups or alternative options — and areas where you don't.

3. **Strengthen Your Resilience:** Identify one area of your life or work where resilience could be improved. For example, create a contingency plan for a critical project or cross-train team members to handle multiple roles.

Key Takeaway

Resilient systems can endure shocks, adapt to change, and recover quickly — assessing and building resilience ensures long-term stability and success.

Chapter 18: Find Balancing Forces

Stability in Opposing Forces

Every system operates within a delicate balance. This balance is maintained by forces that push the system in different directions. These forces act as stabilizers, preventing a system from spiraling out of control or veering into chaos.

Think about your body's internal temperature. When you're too hot, your body sweats to cool down. When you're too cold, you shiver to generate heat. These opposing forces work together to maintain a stable internal temperature — a classic example of a balancing force in action.

Balancing forces are essential for stability, but they can also create resistance to change. For example, in an organization, efforts to introduce innovation might meet balancing forces like established traditions or doubt from employees. Recognizing these forces helps you understand how systems maintain stability and how to work with, rather than against, them.

How to Identify Balancing Forces

1. **Look for Stabilizing Patterns:** Observe areas where the system consistently resists change. For example, are productivity levels in a workplace relatively steady despite fluctuations in workload?

2. **Trace Opposing Forces:** Identify the forces pushing the system in opposite directions. For instance, growth might be balanced by resource limitations or regulatory constraints.

3. **Distinguish Positive and Negative Balancing Forces:** Some balancing forces are beneficial (e.g. quality control processes), while others can stifle progress (e.g. excessive bureaucracy).

4. **Monitor Feedback Loops:** Balancing forces often operate through recursive patterns that self-correct the system, like a thermostat regulating temperature.

Real-World Example

In an economy, inflation is a balancing force for consumer demand. When demand rises too quickly, inflation makes goods more expensive, reducing spending and stabilizing the system. Conversely, when demand falls, prices drop, encouraging spending and boosting the economy. This dynamic helps maintain a balance, preventing extreme booms or busts.

Why It Matters

Balancing forces are the "brakes" that keep systems from going off track. Ignoring them can lead to frustration when efforts to create change meet resistance. But understanding these forces allows you to anticipate challenges, adapt your strategies, and even leverage balancing forces to your advantage. For example, by aligning new initiatives with existing traditions, you can introduce change without disrupting stability.

Exercises

1. **Identify Balancing Forces in Your Life:** Think of a situation where stability is maintained despite external pressures (e.g. a family dynamic or workplace culture). Reflect on what forces are keeping the system balanced.

2. **Outline Opposing Forces:** Choose a project or goal and list the forces pushing for progress and those resisting change. Identify which balancing forces are helpful and which are hindrances.

3. **Work with Balancing Forces:** For a challenge you're facing, brainstorm ways to align your efforts with the system's stabilizing forces instead of working against them.

Key Takeaway

Balancing forces stabilize systems by counteracting change — understanding them helps you work with the system to achieve your goals.

Chapter 19: See Dependencies

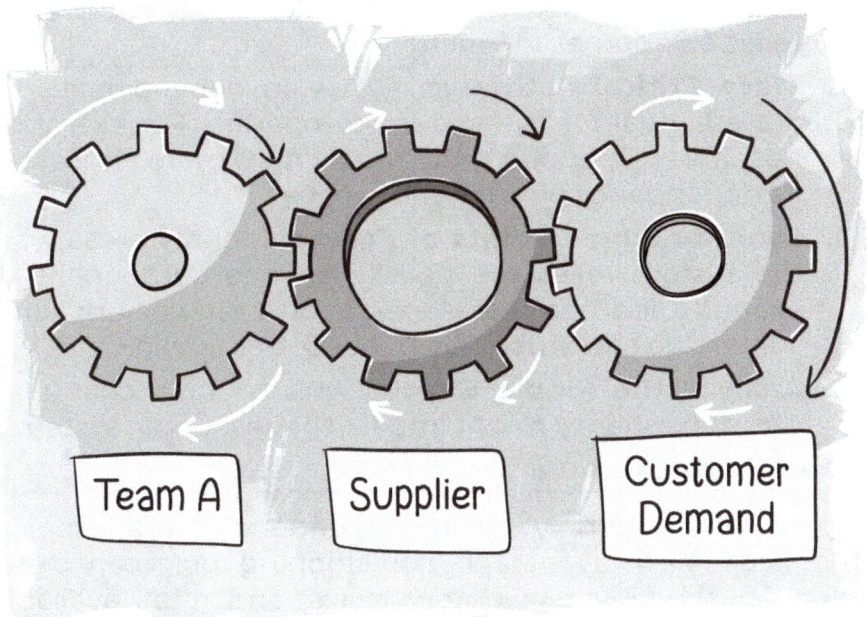

How Systems Rely on Each Other

Systems are built on dependencies. Each part of a system relies on others to function, creating a web of interconnected relationships. Understanding these dependencies is crucial for identifying where a system is strong, where it is vulnerable, and how changes to one part might ripple through the entire system.

Imagine a manufacturing process. The production line depends on a steady supply of materials, skilled workers, and functional machinery. If any of these dependencies fail — say, a supplier misses a delivery — the entire system can grind to a halt. Similarly, in social systems, communities depend on resources like clean water, transportation, and education to thrive.

Dependencies create both opportunities and risks. They enable collaboration and efficiency, but they also make systems fragile if critical dependencies are overlooked or disrupted.

How to Identify Dependencies

1. **Map the System:** Create a diagram of the system's components and connections. Identify where one part relies on another to function.

2. **Trace Critical Pathways:** Focus on dependencies that are essential for the system to operate. For example, a hospital's dependency on electricity is more critical than its dependency on cafeteria services.

3. **Look for Single Points of Failure:** Identify areas where the system relies too heavily on one component. For example, if a business depends on a single supplier, it's vulnerable to disruptions in that supply chain.

4. **Analyze the Ripple Effect:** Consider how changes to one dependency might impact the rest of the system.

Real-World Example

In the global supply chain, dependencies are especially pronounced. A delay at a major shipping port can disrupt production schedules, inventory levels, and retail availability worldwide. Recognizing these dependencies allows businesses to diversify suppliers, build buffer stocks, or improve logistics to reduce vulnerability.

Why It Matters

Dependencies reveal the interdependence of systems. Ignoring them risks overlooking vulnerabilities or underestimating the impact of changes. By identifying dependencies, you can strengthen critical connections, reduce risks, and design systems that are more robust and reliable.

Exercises

1. **Identify Your Dependencies:** Choose a system you rely on (e.g. your work schedule or a household routine). Create a diagram showing how its parts depend on one another. Reflect on which dependencies are most critical.

2. **Spot a Weak Link:** Identify one dependency in your personal or professional life that feels fragile or unreliable. Brainstorm ways to strengthen or replace it.

3. **Assess Ripple Effects:** Think of a recent change in a system you're part of. Trace how that change impacted other components and what this reveals about the system's dependencies.

Key Takeaway

Dependencies are the glue that holds systems together. Understanding them helps you identify strengths, vulnerabilities, and opportunities for improvement.

Chapter 20: Recognize How Systems Change

The Evolution of Systems

No system stays the same forever. Whether it's a natural ecosystem, a business, or a community, systems constantly evolve in response to internal and external pressures. Recognizing how systems change helps you anticipate shifts, adapt to new conditions, and guide systems toward desired outcomes.

System change can occur gradually or suddenly. A forest, for instance, evolves slowly as plants and animals adapt to changing conditions. But a sudden wildfire can trigger rapid transformation, creating opportunities for new species to thrive. Similarly, in organizations, gradual shifts in culture might build over years, while a merger or leadership change can create immediate upheaval.

Understanding how systems change allows you to work with the forces of evolution rather than resisting them.

How to Recognize System Change

1. **Identify Driving Forces:** Look for factors influencing change, such as technology, regulations, or shifting consumer preferences.

2. **Distinguish Gradual from Sudden Change:** Recognize whether the system is evolving incrementally or undergoing a rapid transformation. For example, climate change involves both slow temperature increases and sudden extreme weather events.

3. **Monitor Recursive Patterns:** For example, a growing population creates demand for housing, which drives urban expansion, creating further population growth.

4. **Observe Tipping Points:** Many changes occur when systems cross critical thresholds, leading to rapid shifts in behavior.

Real-World Example

In technology, the adoption of smartphones is a clear example of system change. Gradual improvements in connectivity and affordability prepared the market, but the introduction of app ecosystems caused a tipping point, rapidly transforming industries like communication, entertainment, and commerce.

Why It Matters

Ignoring system change can leave you unprepared for challenges or opportunities. By recognizing how systems evolve, you can anticipate shifts, adapt strategies, and influence outcomes. For example, understanding how consumer habits are changing allows businesses to innovate and stay ahead of competitors.

Exercises

1. **Track Changes in a System:** Choose a system you're part of (e.g. your workplace or a social group). Reflect on how it has changed over the past five years. What forces drove those changes?

2. **Predict Future Changes:** Think of a system you rely on and list factors that might drive change in the next five

years. Consider how you could adapt to or influence these shifts.

3. **Analyze a Sudden Change:** Reflect on a recent event that caused rapid change in your life or work. Identify the tipping point and what enabled the transformation.

Key Takeaway

Systems evolve in response to internal and external forces — recognizing how they change allows you to anticipate, adapt to, and shape their evolution.

Part 2: Analyzing Human-Created Systems

Human-created systems — organizations, economies, communities, and more — are some of the most complex yet familiar systems humans interact with daily. Unlike natural systems, they are influenced by rules, norms, hierarchies, and human behaviors. This section dives into the structures and dynamics that define these systems, equipping you with tools to uncover the forces shaping them, identify their weaknesses, and harness their potential. By mastering these chapters, you'll gain insight into how human systems operate and learn to analyze them with precision and purpose.

Chapter 21: Study Incentive Structures

The Power of Rewards and Penalties

Incentive structures are like the operating system of human-created systems. They're the subtle, often invisible forces that guide how individuals and organizations behave. Incentives come in many forms: financial rewards, social recognition, penalties, or even the promise of autonomy. By understanding these structures, you can decode why people act the way they do and make adjustments to drive desired outcomes.

Consider a workplace environment where employees receive bonuses for meeting sales targets. This incentive motivates employees to focus on closing deals. But what if those deals come at the expense of long-term client satisfaction? Or what if the reward structure inadvertently encourages competition over teamwork? Incentive structures aren't inherently good or bad—they simply drive behavior in whatever direction they're designed to. The challenge lies in ensuring those directions align with the broader goals of the system.

Incentives aren't limited to financial rewards. Social incentives, like public recognition or inclusion in decision-making, can be just as powerful. Negative incentives, such as fines or warnings, also play a role. Together, rewards and penalties create a framework that influences decision-making.

How to Analyze Incentive Structures

1. **Identify Explicit and Implicit Incentives:** Start by listing the formal incentives in the system, such as pay bonuses or performance reviews. Then, dig deeper to uncover implicit ones. For example, does a culture of overworking subtly reward employees who sacrifice personal time?

2. **Trace Behavior Back to Incentives:** Observe how the system's incentives shape specific behaviors. Are employees prioritizing speed over quality? Are citizens complying with recycling programs because of fines or because of social pressure?

3. **Check for Alignment:** Compare the incentives to the system's overarching goals. Are they driving behavior that contributes to long-term success, or do they focus narrowly on short-term gains?

4. **Consider Feedback Loops:** Incentives often create self-reinforcing cycles. For example, rewarding innovation might lead to a culture of experimentation, which in turn produces more innovation.

Real-World Example

In urban transportation, toll roads are designed as a negative incentive to discourage congestion and encourage alternative routes or public transport. But if public transit is unreliable or inaccessible, the toll system can disproportionately affect low-income commuters without achieving its goal. Adjusting the incentive structure — such as reinvesting toll revenue into improving public transport — could better align individual behavior with the system's objectives.

Why It Matters

Incentive structures influence nearly every decision within a system. Ignoring them risks misinterpreting why people behave as they do—or worse, designing systems that unintentionally reward counterproductive actions. By studying incentives, you can align individual motivations with the system's goals, ensuring smoother operations and more sustainable outcomes.

Exercises

1. **List Incentives in Your Life:** Identify explicit incentives (e.g. salary bonuses) and implicit ones (e.g. praise from peers) in your workplace, school, or community. Reflect on how they shape behavior.

2. **Evaluate a Policy's Incentives:** Choose a policy or program, such as recycling incentives or tax credits for electric vehicles. Analyze how its rewards and penalties influence public behavior and whether they achieve the desired outcomes.

3. **Redesign a System's Incentives:** Think of a system you're part of, like a workplace or a team project. Identify a misaligned incentive and propose a way to better align it with the system's objectives.

Key Takeaway

Incentive structures drive behavior in systems — aligning them helps achieve better, long-term outcomes.

Chapter 22: Watch Out for Backfiring Motivators

UNINTENDED CONSEQUENCES

When Good Intentions Backfire

Not all incentives produce the outcomes you expect. Sometimes, a reward or penalty designed to encourage productive behavior has the opposite effect, creating unintended consequences that harm the system. These backfiring motivators are common in human-created systems where complexity often masks how people will react to incentives.

For example, a company that offers bonuses for resolving customer complaints quickly might see employees prioritizing speed over quality. While the intent is to improve customer satisfaction, the actual outcome could be rushed solutions that leave customers dissatisfied. These unintended consequences occur because the incentive focuses on a narrow metric — speed —without accounting for broader goals such as quality or customer trust.

Similarly, fines or penalties can backfire if they unintentionally reinforce undesirable behaviors. A famous example is day-care centers that introduced fines for parents who picked up their children late. Instead of reducing late pickups, the fines made parents feel they were paying for extra time, causing lateness to increase.

How to Identify Backfiring Motivators

1. **Examine Behavioral Side Effects:** Look for unintended behaviors that arise from the incentive. Are people cutting corners, exploiting loopholes, or prioritizing short-term gains over long-term benefits?

2. **Analyze Mismatched Goals:** Consider whether the incentive rewards specific outcomes at the expense of broader system objectives.

3. **Evaluate Feedback Loops:** Some backfiring motivators create patterns that amplify the problem. For example, rewarding individual performance might increase competition while eroding team collaboration.

4. **Test for Perverse Outcomes:** Ask whether the incentive unintentionally encourages the very behavior it's trying to prevent.

Real-World Example

In environmental policy, programs offering subsidies for renewable energy installations often attract companies that prioritize the subsidy over quality. For instance, some solar companies focus on meeting minimum installation criteria to claim subsidies rather than ensuring long-term efficiency. This undermines the program's goal of reducing carbon emissions.

Why It Matters

Backfiring motivators can derail even the best-intentioned systems. Recognizing them allows you to refine incentives and minimize harm. By thinking critically about how people respond to rewards and penalties, you can design systems that encourage desired outcomes without unintended side effects.

Exercises

1. **Reflect on Personal Experience:** Think of a situation where a reward or penalty produced unintended consequences (e.g. rushing to complete a task for a bonus). Analyze what caused the backfire and how it could be corrected.

2. **Evaluate a Policy:** Choose a policy or rule with incentives attached. Identify whether it has backfired and what unintended behaviors it encouraged.

3. **Redesign a Backfiring Incentive:** Identify an incentive in your workplace or community that could backfire. Propose changes to ensure it aligns with long-term goals.

Key Takeaway

Poorly designed incentives can backfire, causing harm instead of progress — analyzing motivators helps you design systems that encourage productive behavior without unintended consequences.

Chapter 23: Track Decision Pathways

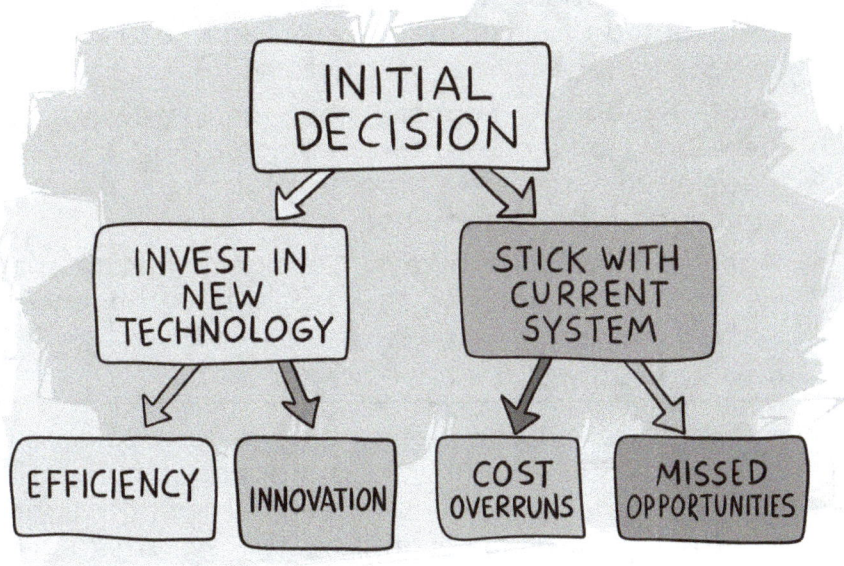

Following the Chain of Choices

Every decision within a system creates a ripple effect, influencing outcomes in ways that aren't always obvious. Decision pathways are the chains of choices that propagate through a system, creating feedback loops, bottlenecks, or opportunities for change. By tracking these pathways, you gain a deeper understanding of how individual choices shape the overall system.

Consider a city deciding whether to invest in public transport or road expansion. Choosing public transport might reduce traffic congestion and emissions, while road expansion could encourage more cars, worsening air quality in the long term. Each decision sets off a cascade of consequences that interact with other parts of the system. Tracking these pathways ensures that decision-makers anticipate both immediate outcomes and downstream effects.

How to Track Decision Pathways

1. **Start with the Initial Decision:** Identify a key decision within the system. What factors influenced it, and who made it?

2. **Determine Subsequent Steps:** Follow how this decision propagated through the system. Did it lead to changes in resources, behaviors, or structures?

3. **Spot Feedback Loops:** Look for pathways where decisions influence future choices. For instance, a decision to automate a process might free up resources, enabling further automation.

4. **Analyze Missed Pathways:** Consider what alternatives weren't chosen and how they might have influenced the system differently.

Real-World Example

In software development, choosing a particular coding framework can shape future decisions about compatibility, scalability, and updates. A poorly chosen framework might lead to long-term technical debt, limiting the system's ability to adapt. Tracking the decision pathway highlights where missteps occurred and how they could have been avoided.

Why It Matters

Understanding decision pathways prevents you from making short-sighted choices. By tracking how decisions ripple through a system, you can anticipate unintended consequences, identify leverage points, and refine future decision-making processes.

Exercises

1. **Track a Personal Decision Pathway:** Reflect on a major decision you made (e.g. pursuing a career path). Outline how that choice influenced subsequent events and opportunities.

2. **Analyze a Group Decision:** Choose a recent team or organizational decision. Trace its pathway and reflect on whether the outcomes aligned with the original intent.

3. **Simulate an Alternative Pathway:** Pick a decision in your workplace or community and imagine an alternative choice. Reflect on how this hypothetical pathway would have changed the system's behavior.

Key Takeaway

Decision pathways reveal how choices shape outcomes — tracking them ensures better decisions and system-wide improvements.

Chapter 24: Examine Rules and Norms

The Frameworks That Shape Systems

Every human-created system is governed by a mix of rules and norms. Rules are the formal, explicit guidelines — laws, policies, or procedures — that define what is allowed and what isn't. Norms, on the other hand, are the informal, often unwritten expectations that emerge from shared behavior, culture, or tradition. Both play critical roles in shaping how systems function, and understanding them is essential for analyzing and improving those systems.

Consider a workplace. Official rules might dictate policies like working hours or performance reviews, but informal norms — such as the expectation to reply to emails after hours — often have just as much influence, if not more. Ignoring these norms can lead to misunderstandings, inefficiencies, or even systemic breakdowns.

Rules and norms interact in powerful ways. Sometimes, they reinforce each other: for example, safety regulations (rules) and a culture of accountability (norms) can together create a strong emphasis on workplace safety. Other times, they conflict: a rule might ban overtime, but a norm of working late could pressure employees to stay after hours anyway. Understanding both frameworks is crucial for diagnosing problems and designing solutions that align with how the system truly operates.

How to Examine Rules and Norms

1. **Distinguish Between Rules and Norms:** Identify which guidelines are formal (e.g. written policies) and which are informal (e.g. social expectations).

2. **Observe Behavior:** Pay attention to how people actually act within the system. Are they following the rules, ignoring them, or adhering more closely to norms?

3. **Look for Conflicts:** Identify where rules and norms might clash. For instance, do policies about collaboration conflict with an individualistic office culture?

4. **Assess Effectiveness:** Consider whether the existing rules and norms are helping or hindering the system's goals. Are outdated rules causing inefficiencies? Are harmful norms holding people back?

Real-World Example

In the education system, official rules might require schools to adhere to strict curricula. However, norms among teachers might emphasize creative, flexible lesson plans. When these norms conflict with rigid rules, it can lead to frustration and burnout for teachers. Resolving such conflicts — perhaps by introducing more flexible policies — can create a better balance between innovation and accountability.

Why It Matters

Rules and norms shape behavior in powerful ways, but they're often misunderstood or overlooked. Ignoring norms can lead to blind spots in how a system operates, while blindly enforcing rules without understanding their effects can create resentment or inefficiency. Examining these frameworks allows you to identify misalignments, resolve conflicts, and design systems that work more effectively.

1. **Identify Rules and Norms in Your Life:** Pick a system you're part of, such as your workplace or a community group. List its formal rules and unwritten norms. Reflect on how they interact.

2. **Spot Conflicts:** Think of a time when a rule conflicted with a norm in your life. How did this tension impact the system, and how might it have been resolved?

3. **Redesign a Rule or Norm:** Identify a rule or norm in a system that feels outdated or ineffective. Propose changes that would better align with the system's goals.

Key Takeaway

Rules and norms define how systems function — analyzing both helps you identify misalignments and improve outcomes.

Chapter 25: Map Communication Channels

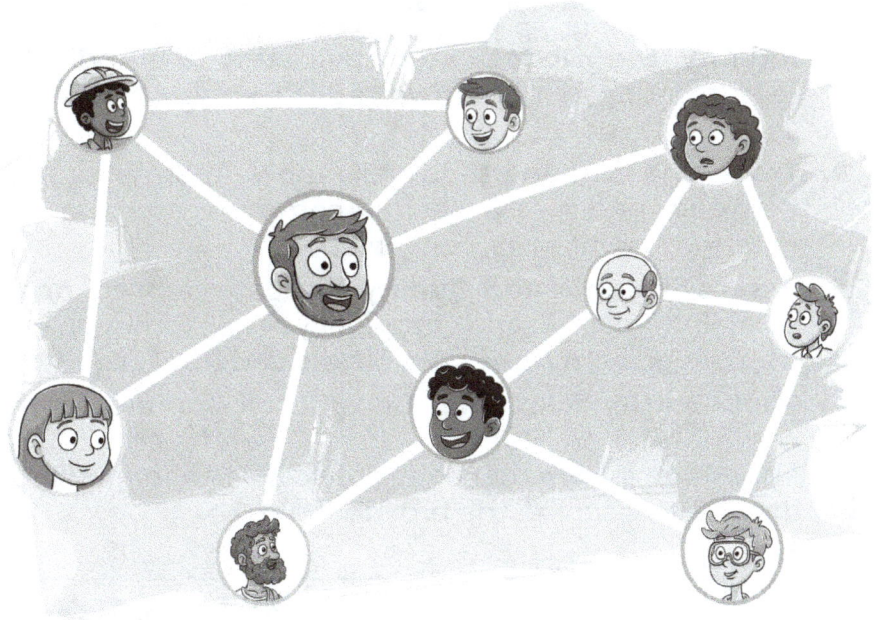

The Lifeblood of Human Systems

Communication is the lifeblood of any human-created system. It's how information flows, decisions are made, and actions are coordinated. But not all communication is created equal. Some channels are strong, consistent, and effective, while others are weak, sporadic, or prone to misinterpretation. Mapping these channels allows you to visualize how information travels through the system, where breakdowns occur, and how communication could be improved.

Imagine a company launching a new product. If communication between marketing and production teams is clear and consistent, the launch is likely to go smoothly. But if communication is sporadic or siloed — if marketing doesn't know production timelines, for example — delays, confusion, and missed opportunities can result.

Communication channels can be formal (e.g. weekly reports or scheduled meetings) or informal (e.g. hallway chats or Slack messages). Both types play important roles, and both need to be understood to improve the flow of information.

How to Map Communication Channels

1. **Identify the Nodes:** Start by listing the individuals, teams, or departments involved in the system. These will serve as the nodes in your map.

2. **Trace the Channels:** Identify how information flows between nodes. Do teams communicate via email, meetings, or informal conversations?

3. **Assess Strength and Quality:** Evaluate each channel for reliability, clarity, and frequency. Are some channels overloaded with noise? Are others underutilized?

4. **Spot Bottlenecks and Gaps:** Look for areas where communication breaks down. For example, does important information get stuck at a managerial level instead of reaching the broader team?

Real-World Example

In large hospitals, effective communication between doctors, nurses, and administrative staff is essential for patient care. Mapping communication channels can reveal inefficiencies, such as a lack of direct communication between doctors and nurses, which might delay critical decisions. Improving these channels—like introducing shared digital records or cross-functional meetings — can streamline care and reduce errors.

Why It Matters

Poor communication is one of the most common reasons systems fail. Information bottlenecks, misinterpretations, or missing channels can lead to wasted time, costly mistakes, or even systemic breakdowns. By mapping and improving communication channels, you can ensure that information flows smoothly and the system operates more efficiently.

Exercises

1. **Map Your Communication Network:** Choose a system you're part of, like a workplace or a social group. Create a diagram showing how information flows between its components. Reflect on where communication is strong and where it's weak.

2. **Spot Bottlenecks:** Think of a time when poor communication caused problems. What channel broke down, and how could it have been improved?

3. **Redesign a Communication Channel:** Identify a weak communication channel in a system you're part of. Propose a way to strengthen it, such as introducing clearer protocols or using better tools.

Key Takeaway

Communication channels are essential for the smooth operation of systems. Mapping and improving them prevents breakdowns and enhances outcomes.

Chapter 26: Notice Bottlenecks

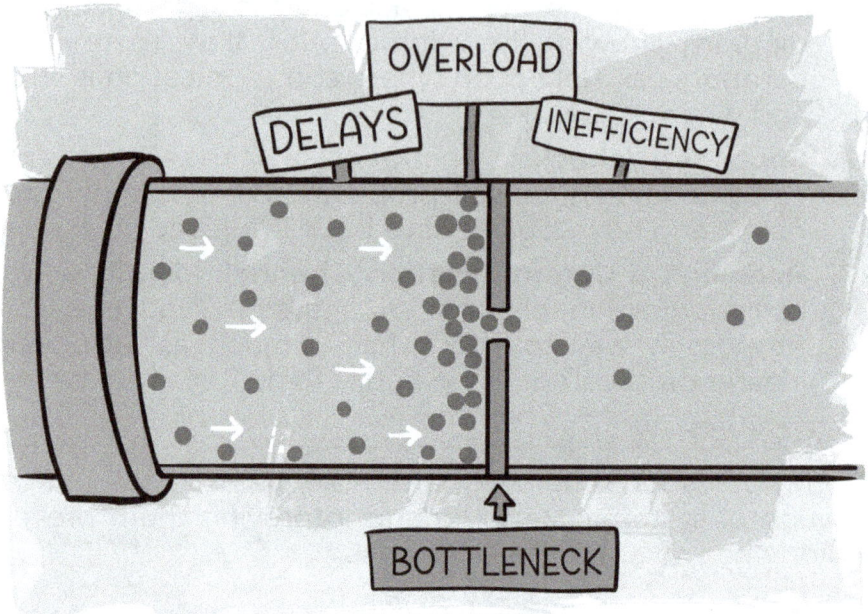

Where the Flow Slows Down

In any system, bottlenecks are points where flows — whether of resources, information, or work — get stuck or slowed. They act like a clogged artery in a circulatory system, disrupting the entire system's efficiency and capacity. Identifying and addressing bottlenecks is one of the most effective ways to improve performance and ensure smooth operation.

For example, in a supply chain, a bottleneck might occur at a manufacturing plant that can't meet demand. The delay at this point affects the entire chain, leading to late deliveries, frustrated customers, and lost revenue. Similarly, in a team project, a bottleneck might be a single overworked individual responsible for approving every decision.

Bottlenecks aren't always obvious. They often hide within layers of processes or routines, their effects rippling outward in ways that mask the root cause. By pinpointing these constrictions, you can unlock greater efficiency and improve outcomes across the system.

How to Identify Bottlenecks

1. **Track the Flow:** Start by visualizing how resources, tasks, or information move through the system. Look for stages where progress slows or stops.

2. **Measure Wait Times:** Bottlenecks often create delays. Identify areas where tasks or resources spend the most time waiting to move forward.

3. **Analyze Overloaded Points:** Look for components of the system that consistently operate at or beyond their capacity. For instance, is one team overwhelmed while others are underutilized?

4. **Observe Downstream Effects:** Bottlenecks often cause ripple effects, such as missed deadlines or errors in later stages. Trace these problems back to their source.

Real-World Example

In healthcare, emergency rooms are often bottlenecks in hospital systems. Patients may wait hours for a doctor because beds are full, diagnostics are delayed, or specialists are unavailable. These bottlenecks affect the entire hospital, reducing overall efficiency and patient satisfaction. Addressing them — by streamlining patient triage, increasing staff capacity, or improving communication — can transform the system.

Why It Matters

Bottlenecks reduce the capacity of the entire system. Even if every other part of the system operates efficiently, a single bottleneck can limit output, create frustration, and inflate costs. By identifying and addressing these constrictions, you can unlock the system's full potential and create more reliable, scalable processes.

Exercises

1. **Identify a Bottleneck in Your Life:** Think of a recurring task or process (e.g. preparing for meetings or completing a household chore). Pinpoint where progress consistently slows down and why.

2. **Map a Workflow:** Choose a system you interact with, such as a workplace process. Sketch out the flow of tasks and identify where delays or backlogs occur.

3. **Brainstorm Solutions:** For a bottleneck you've identified, list potential solutions, such as redistributing work, automating tasks, or simplifying approvals.

Key Takeaway

Bottlenecks slow down systems and limit their potential — identifying and addressing them improves efficiency and unlocks new capacity.

Chapter 27: Identify System Archetypes

The Blueprint of Systems

Systems, despite their complexity, often follow familiar patterns. These recurring structures, called system archetypes, help explain why systems behave the way they do. Identifying these archetypes allows you to anticipate outcomes, diagnose problems, and design smarter interventions.

One classic archetype is "Success to the Successful." In this structure, resources flow disproportionately to those already succeeding, creating a feedback loop that reinforces their advantage. Think of educational funding: well-funded schools produce better results, attracting more funding, while underfunded schools struggle to improve. Another common archetype is "Shifting the Burden," where short-term fixes address symptoms but ignore root causes. For example, relying on overtime to meet deadlines instead of improving workflow efficiency.

By recognizing archetypes, you can simplify complex systems and identify leverage points where small changes have big impacts.

How to Identify System Archetypes

1. **Look for Feedback Loops:** Many archetypes involve reinforcing or balancing loops. For instance, a loop might reinforce growth (e.g. word-of-mouth promotion) or maintain stability (e.g. thermostat regulation).

2. **Analyze Recurring Problems:** Patterns of recurring challenges — like resource inequalities or declining performance—often signal an underlying archetype.

3. **Match Behaviors to Archetypes:** Compare the system's behavior to common archetypes, such as "Limits to Growth," where expansion eventually hits a constraint, or "Fixes That Fail," where solutions create new problems.

4. **Identify Root Causes:** Archetypes often reveal deeper issues driving system behavior. For example, in "Escalation," competition between two actors leads to mutually destructive behavior.

Real-World Example

A company experiencing high turnover might fall into the "Fixes That Fail" archetype. To address staff departures, it increases recruitment efforts rather than addressing the root cause of dissatisfaction. Over time, turnover continues, and recruitment costs escalate. Recognizing this archetype enables leaders to focus on improving workplace culture instead of relying on short-term fixes.

Why It Matters

System archetypes simplify complexity, revealing the recurring structures that drive system behavior. By identifying these patterns, you can anticipate problems, avoid ineffective solutions, and target interventions where they will have the most impact.

Exercises

1. **Spot an Archetype in Your Life:** Think of a recurring problem in a system you interact with (e.g. a work process or family routine). Identify whether it matches

an archetype, such as "Shifting the Burden" or "Escalation."

2. **Outline a Feedback Loop:** Choose a system and map its feedback loops. Determine whether they are reinforcing (driving growth or decline) or balancing (maintaining stability).

3. **Break the Pattern:** For a system archetype you've identified, brainstorm ways to intervene and disrupt the pattern. For example, how can you address the root cause in a "Fixes That Fail" structure?

Key Takeaway

System archetypes reveal recurring patterns of behavior — understanding them allows you to diagnose problems and design effective solutions.

Chapter 28: Explore Power Bases

Who Holds the Power?

Power is the force that drives decisions, shapes relationships, and determines resource allocation within human-created systems. But power is not always where it seems to be. While formal authority represents one kind of power, informal power bases often have equal or greater influence. These hidden forces can include subject-matter expertise, control over critical resources, social connections, or even sheer charisma.

Exploring power bases allows you to identify where influence truly lies, how decisions are shaped, and how to build strategies that align with these dynamics. Whether you're working to implement change, resolve conflicts, or simply understand a system, recognizing power bases ensures you can act effectively and with foresight.

How to Explore Power Bases

1. **Identify Formal Power:** Start by visualizing explicit authority in the system — individuals or groups with official titles or positions. This could include CEOs,

policymakers, or project managers who are empowered by organizational structures to make decisions.

2. **Uncover Informal Power:** Look for people who, despite lacking formal authority, influence outcomes through expertise, social connections, or credibility. Informal power often lies with individuals who others seek out for advice, support, or resources.

3. **Trace Resource Control:** Power is closely tied to control over key resources — money, knowledge, tools, or networks. For example, a department controlling a critical budget might have outsized influence even if its official rank is lower in the hierarchy.

4. **Analyze Relationships:** Power flows through relationships. Observe alliances, rivalries, and networks to see how influence is distributed. For example, in a team project, an unofficial leader might emerge due to their ability to mediate conflicts and rally others.

Real-World Example

Consider a local government planning a community development project. The mayor holds formal power to approve the budget and make high-level decisions. However, a long-standing community leader with no official role might wield more influence because of their relationships with residents and their deep understanding of local needs. Ignoring this informal power base could lead to public resistance, even if the mayor's plan is sound. Recognizing the leader's influence allows for collaboration and greater alignment with community priorities.

Why It Matters

Power bases dictate how systems operate, who gets heard, and how change happens. Failing to recognize informal power can derail well-intentioned plans, create unnecessary conflict, or limit the system's ability to adapt. Conversely, understanding both formal and informal power enables you to anticipate resistance, build coalitions, and ensure solutions are accepted and implemented.

For example, if you're leading a project and focus solely on the formal hierarchy, you might miss the opportunity to engage informal influencers who can help rally the team. Similarly, in a negotiation, understanding who controls key resources allows you to target your efforts where they will have the most impact.

Exercises

1. **Map Power in a System You Know:** Think of a system you're part of, such as your workplace or a community group. Identify the individuals or groups with formal authority and those with informal influence. Reflect on how their power shapes decisions and outcomes.

2. **Trace Resource Control:** Pick a system and analyze who controls its key resources, such as budgets, information, or tools. How does resource control affect the flow of power?

3. **Navigate Power Dynamics:** For a challenge you're facing, consider how power is distributed. Who do you need to engage or influence to achieve your goal? How can you align your approach with the system's power dynamics?

Key Takeaway

Power is a combination of formal authority, resource control, and informal influence. Understanding these dynamics allows you to navigate systems more effectively and achieve lasting results.

Chapter 29: Find Leverage Points

Small Actions, Big Impacts

In complex systems, not all actions have equal weight. Some points within the system — known as leverage points — hold disproportionate influence over its behavior. Identifying and acting on these points allows you to create meaningful change with minimal effort, avoiding wasted energy on areas that yield little impact.

For example, consider a city trying to reduce traffic congestion. Building more roads might seem like a logical solution, but it often encourages more car usage, worsening the problem over time. A better leverage point might be investing in affordable public transit. By changing how people move through the system, this single intervention can alleviate congestion, reduce emissions, and improve urban mobility.

Leverage points are not always obvious. They often exist at deeper levels of the system, such as the underlying rules, goals, or feedback loops, rather than at surface-level processes. Finding these points requires a deep understanding of how the system operates and where small changes can trigger larger, cascading effects.

How to Identify Leverage Points

1. **Define the System:** Start by visualizing the system's components and connections. Identify areas where influence flows through multiple parts of the system.

2. **Analyze Feedback Loops:** Feedback loops—whether reinforcing or balancing—are often powerful leverage points. For example, amplifying a positive feedback loop can drive growth, while interrupting a negative loop can stabilize the system.

3. **Focus on Underlying Structures:** Leverage points are often found in the system's foundational rules, norms, or goals. Ask: What structural changes could shift the system's behavior?

4. **Test Small Changes:** Experiment with small interventions in different parts of the system. Observe which ones create the greatest ripple effects.

Real-World Example

In public health, childhood vaccination programs serve as a critical leverage point. By immunizing children against preventable diseases, these programs reduce illness, decrease healthcare costs, and improve long-term societal health. This single intervention has a far-reaching impact, benefiting both individuals and the broader system.

Why It Matters

Without understanding leverage points, efforts to improve systems often focus on surface-level symptoms rather than root causes. This can lead to wasted resources or unintended consequences. By targeting leverage points, you maximize impact while minimizing effort, making your interventions more efficient and effective.

For instance, a company struggling with low employee morale might initially focus on superficial fixes like team-building activities. However, identifying a deeper leverage point — such as improving leadership communication — can create a lasting cultural shift that boosts morale across the organization.

Exercises

1. **Identify a Leverage Point in Your Life:** Think of a recurring issue, such as managing your time or improving teamwork. What small change could have a large, positive impact?

2. **Map a System for Leverage Points:** Choose a system you interact with (e.g. a work process or a family routine). Identify areas where small interventions could create significant improvements.

3. **Experiment with Leverage:** Test a small change in a system, such as streamlining a single step in a workflow. Observe how this impacts the larger system.

Key Takeaway

Leverage points are areas where small actions create big changes — identifying and targeting these points allows you to maximize impact and efficiency.

Chapter 30: Trace Resource Inequalities

The Uneven Distribution of Resources

In human-created systems, resources are rarely distributed evenly. Whether it's wealth, access to education, or even time, these inequalities shape how systems function, often creating imbalances that perpetuate themselves over time. Tracing resource inequalities allows you to understand where these imbalances exist, how they affect the system, and what changes could create more equitable outcomes.

Take the example of a school system. Schools in wealthy neighborhoods often have better funding, smaller class sizes, and more extracurricular programs. Meanwhile, schools in underprivileged areas struggle with larger class sizes, fewer resources, and less experienced teachers. These inequalities create feedback loops: better-funded schools produce higher-achieving students, attracting more funding, while underfunded schools fall further behind.

Understanding resource inequalities isn't just about identifying disparities — it's about recognizing how those disparities shape the system's behavior and finding ways to address them.

How to Trace Resource Inequalities

1. **Identify Key Resources:** Start by listing the critical resources within the system, such as money, time, information, or access to services.

2. **Structure Distribution:** Visualize how these resources are distributed among different parts of the system. Are some groups, departments, or individuals receiving significantly more or less than others?

3. **Trace Causes:** Investigate why these inequalities exist. Are they the result of historical decisions, structural biases, or external constraints?

4. **Analyze Impacts:** Consider how resource inequalities affect system behavior. For instance, do they create bottlenecks, reinforce negative feedback loops, or limit opportunities for growth?

Real-World Example

In global development, resource inequalities are starkly visible. Wealthy countries have access to advanced healthcare, infrastructure, and education, while poorer nations struggle with basic necessities. These disparities perpetuate cycles of poverty and hinder global progress. Addressing these inequalities through targeted interventions — such as international aid or fair trade agreements — can create more balanced and sustainable systems.

Why It Matters

Resource inequalities create inefficiencies, limit opportunities, and reinforce systemic disadvantages. Ignoring these disparities can lead to short-term fixes that fail to address underlying problems. By tracing resource inequalities, you can design interventions that redistribute resources more equitably, improving outcomes for the entire system.

For example, in a workplace, an overworked team might struggle to meet deadlines while other teams have excess capacity. Redistributing workloads and resources not only improves team performance but also enhances overall productivity.

Exercises

1. **Identify Inequalities in Your Life:** Think of a system you're part of, such as your workplace or community. Where do you see disparities in resources like time, information, or support?

2. **Pinpoint a Resource Gap:** Choose a system and create a visual map of its resource distribution. Highlight areas of abundance and scarcity.

3. **Propose a Redistribution Strategy:** For a resource inequality you've identified, brainstorm ways to redistribute resources more equitably. What steps could you take to make the system fairer?

Key Takeaway

Resource inequalities shape how systems function. Addressing these disparities can create more equitable and effective outcomes.

Chapter 31: Spot Structural Biases

The Invisible Tilt of Systems

Every human-created system has built-in structures — rules, policies, cultural norms, and historical contexts — that shape its behavior. Sometimes, these structures create biases that advantage some groups while disadvantaging others. Unlike personal bias, structural bias is embedded within the system itself, influencing outcomes regardless of individual intentions.

For example, consider hiring practices. A company might genuinely want a diverse workforce, but if its job advertisements use jargon that appeals to a narrow demographic, or if its recruitment relies on referrals from current employees (who are demographically similar), structural biases limit who applies and gets hired. These biases don't stem from deliberate exclusion but from how the system is designed.

Spotting structural biases requires looking at how the system operates beneath the surface. It's not about blaming individuals but understanding the frameworks that perpetuate inequality, inefficiency, or unfairness — and finding ways to make the system more equitable.

How to Spot Structural Biases

1. **Examine Outcomes:** Start by analyzing who benefits and who doesn't from the system. For example, do certain groups consistently have better access to resources or opportunities?

2. **Trace the Rules:** Look at the formal policies or informal norms that guide decision-making. Are there policies that unintentionally exclude or disadvantage certain groups?

3. **Consider Historical Contexts:** Many structural biases are rooted in historical inequalities. For instance, systemic disparities in education or housing can stem from policies enacted decades ago.

4. **Analyze Access Points:** Determine whether all participants have equal access to the system's benefits. Are there barriers—such as costs, language, or geography—that prevent equitable participation?

Real-World Example

In healthcare, structural biases often manifest in unequal access to services. Rural communities, for instance, might lack nearby hospitals, forcing residents to travel long distances for care. This geographic bias creates disparities in health outcomes, even though the healthcare system itself may aim to serve everyone equally. Addressing this bias requires systemic changes, such as investing in telemedicine or rural health facilities.

Why It Matters

Structural biases create systemic inefficiencies and inequities. They prevent the system from reaching its full potential by limiting participation or concentrating benefits among a few. Ignoring these biases perpetuates inequality, while addressing them can unlock new opportunities and make the system more inclusive and effective.

For instance, a workplace that actively identifies and reduces structural biases — by standardizing interviews or offering remote work options — can attract a more diverse talent pool, leading to innovation and better team performance.

Exercises

1. **Spot Structural Biases in Your Life:** Identify a system you interact with (e.g. a workplace or educational program). Look for disparities in outcomes and consider what structural factors might contribute.

2. **Analyze a Policy or Rule:** Choose a formal policy or rule in a system you know. Reflect on whether it unintentionally creates barriers or advantages for certain groups.

3. **Propose a Systemic Change:** For a structural bias you've identified, brainstorm ways to redesign the system to make it more equitable, such as revising eligibility criteria or creating new access points.

Key Takeaway

Structural biases are ingrained in systems. Identifying and addressing them leads to fairer and more effective results.

Chapter 32: Understand The Snowball Effect

How Small Changes Become Big Shifts

In many systems, a small change can set off a chain reaction that grows in scale and impact. This is called the snowball effect. Understanding this dynamic helps you anticipate exponential growth or decline and design interventions that harness or counteract it.

For example, in personal finance, saving a small amount of money each month can snowball into substantial savings over years due to compound interest. Conversely, in social media, a single post can go viral if enough people share it early, triggering a cascade of visibility and engagement. The snowball effect can drive growth, innovation, or progress, but it can also amplify problems if left unchecked.

Recognizing when and where snowball effects occur allows you to influence systems more strategically, either by nurturing positive changes or intervening before negative dynamics spiral out of control.

How to Understand The Snowball Effect

1. **Identify Reinforcing Loops:** Look for areas where a small input amplifies itself through feedback, such as word-of-mouth promotion or recurring customer loyalty.

2. **Trace the Starting Point:** Pinpoint the initial change or trigger that sets the snowball in motion. For instance, what prompted a sudden spike in product demand?

3. **Monitor Acceleration:** Snowball effects often begin slowly but grow exponentially. Observe where growth or change accelerates, and identify whether it's beneficial or harmful.

4. **Intervene Early:** If a snowball effect is creating negative outcomes, the best time to intervene is in the early stages, before it gains momentum.

Real-World Example

In environmental systems, deforestation can create a snowball effect. Cutting down trees reduces carbon absorption, contributing to climate change, which in turn accelerates deforestation through droughts or wildfires. Addressing this cycle requires interventions like reforestation programs to slow or reverse the snowball effect before it causes irreversible damage.

Why It Matters

The snowball effect explains why systems can change so rapidly and dramatically. Ignoring these dynamics can leave you unprepared for exponential growth or decline. By understanding and leveraging the snowball effect, you can design systems that amplify positive outcomes, mitigate risks, and create long-lasting impacts.

For example, a company launching a new product might focus on creating early momentum through targeted marketing, knowing that an initial burst of adoption can snowball into widespread popularity. Similarly, addressing small problems early — like a minor error in a workflow — prevents them from escalating into larger crises.

Exercises

1. **Identify a Snowball Effect:** Think of a system where small changes have grown into significant outcomes (e.g. a viral trend or a growing habit). Reflect on what caused the snowball effect.

2. **Create a Feedback Pattern:** Choose a system and identify a reinforcing loop that creates a snowball effect. Consider how this loop could be nurtured or disrupted.

3. **Design a Snowball Strategy:** For a project or goal you're working on, brainstorm ways to create a snowball effect. What small actions could trigger exponential growth or progress?

Key Takeaway

The snowball effect demonstrates how small actions can rapidly escalate — recognizing this process helps you magnify positive changes and tackle issues before they grow.

Chapter 33: Analyze Network Centrality

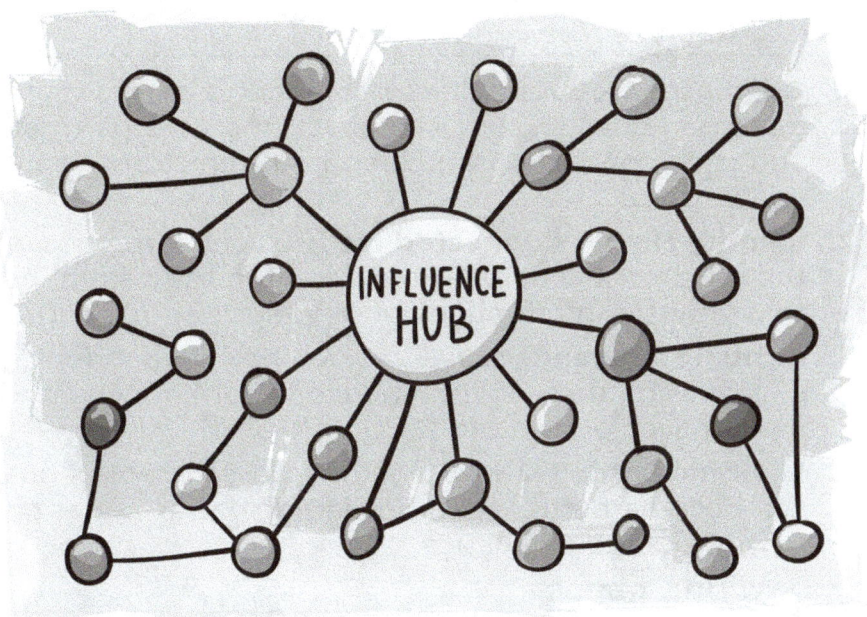

The Power of Central Nodes

In any system, some parts are more connected and influential than others. These highly connected nodes are referred to as "central nodes," and their position in the network makes them critical to the system's operation. Understanding network centrality helps you identify which nodes are essential for maintaining the system's structure, which ones facilitate communication, and which ones could cause major disruption if removed.

Think of a social network: a central influencer with a large number of connections can amplify information quickly, whereas a less connected individual has limited reach. Similarly, in an organizational structure, a department that serves as the hub for communication between other teams holds significant influence over workflows and outcomes.

Central nodes aren't always obvious. They might not hold formal authority or dominate resources, but their position in the network makes them pivotal. By analyzing network centrality, you can uncover hidden influencers, anticipate vulnerabilities, and strategically target interventions.

How to Analyze Network Centrality

1. **Define the Network:** Start by creating a diagram of the system's nodes (e.g. individuals, teams, or departments) and their connections. Include both direct and indirect relationships.

2. **Identify Highly Connected Nodes:** Look for nodes with the most connections. These are often the central hubs that facilitate information flow and decision-making.

3. **Evaluate Dependency:** Consider how dependent the system is on these central nodes. What happens if they are removed or disrupted?

4. **Look for Bottlenecks:** Sometimes, overly central nodes can become bottlenecks, slowing down the system due to their outsized influence.

Real-World Example

In supply chains, distribution hubs often serve as central nodes. For instance, a major shipping port connects suppliers, manufacturers, and distributors worldwide. Disruptions at these central nodes — like a port strike or a natural disaster — can ripple across the entire supply chain, causing delays and shortages.

Why It Matters

Central nodes are both strengths and vulnerabilities in a system. Their connectivity makes them indispensable for efficiency and coordination, but it also means that disruptions at these points can have outsized effects. By analyzing network centrality, you can protect critical nodes, improve their functionality, or design systems that are less reliant on single points of failure.

For example, in an organization, central nodes like project managers can facilitate communication across teams. However, if all information flows through one individual, their absence (e.g. due to illness) can create delays. Building redundancy — such as empowering multiple people to handle communication — reduces this vulnerability.

Exercises

1. **Map a Network You Know:** Choose a network you interact with, like your workplace or a social group. Identify the central nodes and reflect on their role in the system.

2. **Analyze Dependency:** For a system you're part of, consider how dependent it is on its central nodes. What would happen if one of these nodes failed?

3. **Strengthen a Network:** Identify a central node in a system you know. Brainstorm ways to either reduce dependency on this node or enhance its functionality.

Key Takeaway

Network centrality reveals the critical nodes that influence system behavior — analyzing these hubs helps you strengthen systems and reduce vulnerabilities.

Chapter 34: Look for Cross-System Overlaps

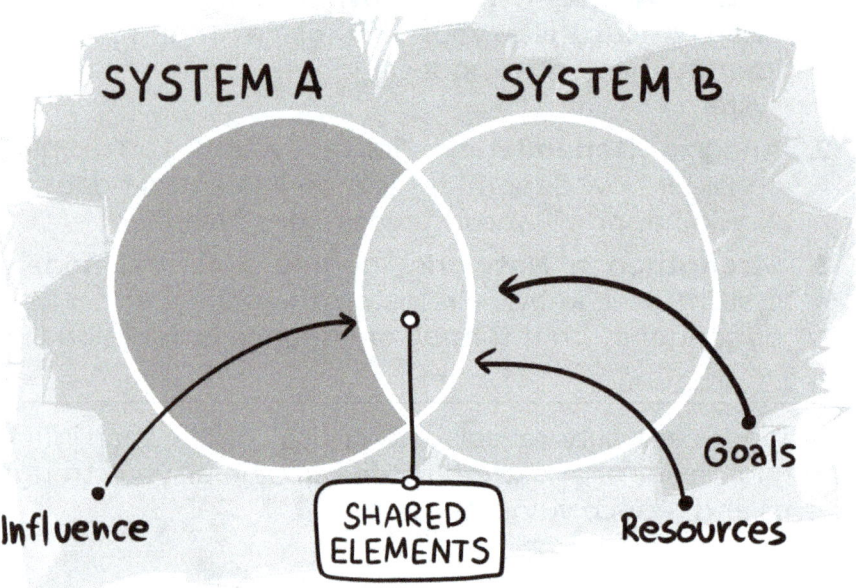

When Systems Intersect

No system exists in isolation. Human-created systems often overlap with or depend on other systems, sharing resources, goals, or elements that influence one another. Recognizing these cross-system overlaps allows you to see how interconnected systems shape behavior, create dependencies, and amplify outcomes.

Consider urban transportation systems and housing policies. The two might seem separate, but they're deeply interconnected. Affordable housing near public transit hubs reduces commute times, improves access to jobs, and reduces congestion. Ignoring this overlap can lead to poorly integrated systems that fail to meet the needs of the people they serve.

Cross-system overlaps often create opportunities for synergy but can also introduce risks. Identifying and understanding these overlaps ensures that you can leverage their strengths and mitigate potential conflicts.

How to Identify Cross-System Overlaps

1. **Map the Systems:** Start by outlining the individual systems you're analyzing. Look for areas where they share resources, influence each other, or have overlapping goals.

2. **Analyze Shared Elements:** Focus on the areas of overlap. Are the systems competing for the same resources, or are they working together to achieve complementary objectives?

3. **Consider Cascading Effects:** Changes in one system often impact the other. For example, how do changes in an education system affect the local labor market?

4. **Leverage Synergies:** Look for ways the systems can support each other. For example, aligning health programs with community centers can improve access to care.

Real-World Example

In disaster response, emergency management systems overlap with healthcare, transportation, and communication networks. A well-coordinated response relies on understanding how these systems interact—for example, ensuring that roads are clear for ambulances and that hospitals have the resources they need to handle surges of patients.

Why It Matters

Ignoring cross-system overlaps can lead to inefficiencies, conflicts, or missed opportunities. By recognizing these intersections, you can design solutions that work across systems, achieving better outcomes with fewer resources. For example, integrating public health initiatives with education systems can improve awareness and outcomes in both areas.

Conversely, poorly managed overlaps can create cascading failures. If an energy grid and transportation network are poorly integrated, a blackout could disrupt public transit, creating widespread chaos. Identifying and addressing these vulnerabilities ensures greater system resilience.

Exercises

1. **Identify an Overlap:** Think of two systems you interact with (e.g. work processes and team communication). Where do they overlap, and how does this affect outcomes?

2. **Lay Out Shared Elements:** Choose two overlapping systems and list the resources, goals, or dependencies they share. Reflect on whether these overlaps create opportunities or risks.

3. **Leverage Synergies:** For a pair of systems you know, brainstorm ways to improve their integration. How can better alignment enhance outcomes for both?

Key Takeaway

Cross-system overlaps reveal shared elements and dependencies. Understanding them allows you to design more integrated, efficient, and resilient solutions.

Chapter 35: Track Failures to Learn

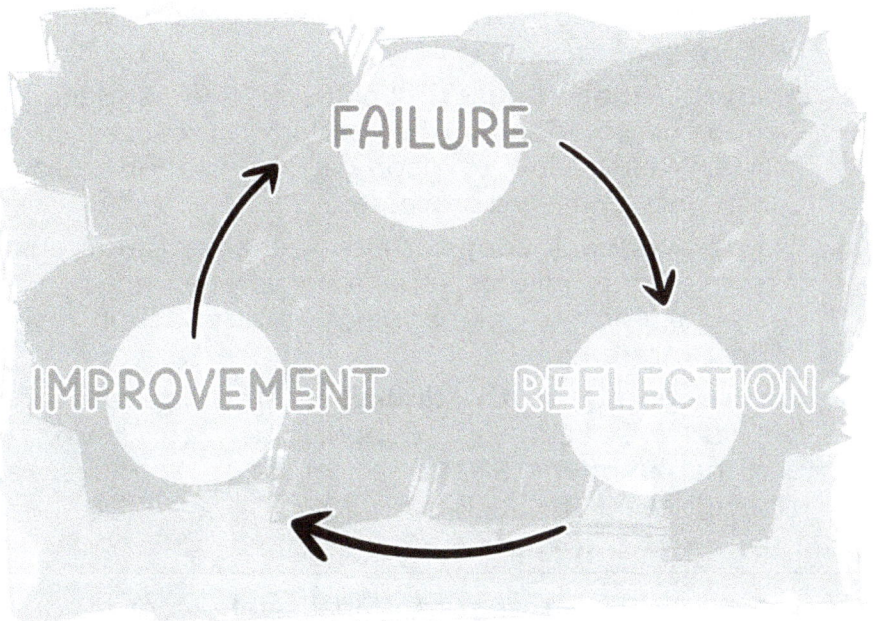

The Value of Failure

Failures are inevitable in any human-created system. However, what distinguishes high-performing systems from struggling ones is their ability to learn from these failures. When systems fail to reflect on mistakes, they're doomed to repeat them. Tracking failures to learn ensures that each setback becomes a stepping stone toward improvement, not a permanent obstacle.

Consider product recalls in manufacturing. A company that identifies the root cause—such as a flaw in the production line—can redesign its processes to prevent future issues. A company that ignores the failure might face repeated recalls, damaging its reputation and profitability.

Failures aren't just opportunities to fix mistakes; they're windows into the system's vulnerabilities. By analyzing these moments, you can uncover deeper issues, anticipate future risks, and strengthen the system as a whole.

How to Track Failures to Learn

1. **Document Failures:** Keep a record of failures, including what happened, why it happened, and what the outcomes were.

2. **Analyze Root Causes:** Look beyond surface-level symptoms to identify the underlying causes of the failure. Was it due to poor communication, resource constraints, or flawed processes?

3. **Create Feedback Loops:** Build mechanisms that ensure lessons from failures are incorporated into future decisions. For example, implement after-action reviews or post-mortems.

4. **Encourage a Growth Mindset:** Foster a culture where failures are seen as opportunities to learn, not punishable offenses. This encourages openness and innovation.

Real-World Example

In aviation, the industry's exceptional safety record is due to its rigorous approach to learning from failures. Every accident or near-miss is thoroughly investigated, with findings shared across airlines and manufacturers. This culture of learning has led to continuous improvements in technology, training, and safety protocols.

Why It Matters

Failures are some of the most valuable data points in a system. Ignoring them leads to repeated mistakes, wasted resources, and unnecessary risks. Tracking failures to learn ensures that each misstep drives growth and resilience, transforming short-term setbacks into long-term progress.

For instance, a software development team that regularly reviews project failures can improve workflows, prevent bugs, and deliver better products. In contrast, a team that avoids addressing failures risks creating technical debt and missed deadlines.

Exercises

1. **Reflect on a Recent Failure:** Think of a failure you experienced in a system (e.g. a missed deadline or a flawed project). What lessons did you take from it, and how could the system improve?

2. **Conduct a Root Cause Analysis:** Choose a failure in your workplace or community and dig into its root causes. What underlying issues contributed, and how can they be addressed?

3. **Design a Feedback Loop:** For a system you're part of, propose a way to ensure failures are regularly analyzed and their lessons implemented.

Key Takeaway

Failures are opportunities for learning. Tracking them allows systems to grow, adapt, and become more resilient over time.

Chapter 36: Identify Siloed Thinking

The Isolation Problem

Siloed thinking occurs when parts of a system operate in isolation, focusing narrowly on their own goals without considering how their actions affect the broader system. This mindset can emerge in teams, departments, or even entire organizations, creating inefficiencies, redundancies, and missed opportunities for collaboration.

Imagine a large organization where the marketing, sales, and product teams work independently. The marketing team launches campaigns without consulting the product team, leading to an influx of customers for a feature still in development. Meanwhile, the sales team, unaware of these efforts, misses opportunities to align their pitch. Each team might feel it's doing its job well, but the lack of coordination creates chaos at the system level.

Siloed thinking is one of the most common barriers to system-wide efficiency. Identifying and addressing it is crucial for unlocking the system's full potential.

How to Identify Siloed Thinking

1. **Look for Isolated Goals:** Check whether different parts of the system have conflicting or disconnected objectives. Are teams pursuing their own KPIs without aligning with broader goals?

2. **Trace Information Flows:** Siloed systems often have poor communication channels. Identify where information gets stuck or fails to reach key stakeholders.

3. **Analyze Duplication of Effort:** Siloed thinking often leads to redundant work. For example, are two teams solving the same problem independently without realizing it?

4. **Watch for Blame Shifting:** In siloed systems, problems are often passed between teams, with little ownership or collaboration to resolve them.

Real-World Example

In healthcare, siloed thinking often occurs between different departments in a hospital. A patient might receive care from several specialists who don't coordinate, leading to redundant tests, conflicting advice, and delayed treatment. Integrated care models address this issue by fostering collaboration and information sharing across departments, improving outcomes and efficiency.

Why It Matters

Siloed thinking prevents systems from functioning as cohesive units. It wastes resources, creates delays, and leads to suboptimal outcomes. Addressing this mindset promotes collaboration, increases efficiency, and ensures that all parts of the system work toward shared goals.

For instance, an organization that breaks down silos between its marketing and product teams can align campaigns with actual product availability, boosting customer satisfaction and revenue. Similarly, in government, breaking down silos between agencies enables more coordinated and effective policy implementation.

Exercises

1. **Spot Silos in Your Life:** Think of a system you're part of (e.g. your workplace or a community group). Identify where siloed thinking might exist and how it affects outcomes.

2. **Trace Communication Gaps:** Choose a system and sketch out its communication flows. Highlight areas where information doesn't travel freely and consider how to improve these connections.

3. **Propose a Collaboration Strategy:** For a siloed system you've identified, suggest ways to improve collaboration. For example, introduce cross-functional meetings or shared goals.

Key Takeaway

Siloed thinking isolates parts of a system. Breaking down these barriers fosters collaboration and improves outcomes.

Chapter 37: Evaluate the Role of Middle Actors

The Connectors in the System

Middle actors, or intermediaries, are the connectors in a system. They bridge gaps between different components, ensuring resources, information, or influence flow smoothly. While often overlooked, these actors are essential for keeping the system functional.

Consider a supply chain: distributors act as middle actors, linking manufacturers to retailers. Without their role, products would have no efficient path to market. Similarly, in social systems, middle actors might include community leaders who translate government policies into actionable programs for local residents.

Middle actors are not just conduits — they often shape how the system operates. They can act as gatekeepers, amplifiers, or even bottlenecks. Understanding their role allows you to identify opportunities for optimization and ensure the system runs smoothly.

How to Evaluate the Role of Middle Actors

1. **Identify Key Intermediaries:** Map the system and highlight the individuals, teams, or entities that connect different parts.

2. **Analyze Their Functions:** What role do these middle actors play? Are they facilitators, decision-makers, or gatekeepers?

3. **Assess Their Impact:** Consider how effectively the middle actors perform their role. Do they accelerate workflows, or do they create bottlenecks?

4. **Examine Power Dynamics:** Middle actors often have significant influence over the system. Evaluate whether they use this influence to support or hinder the system's goals.

Real-World Example

In energy systems, utilities serve as middle actors between power generators and consumers. Their role goes beyond simple distribution—they manage demand, maintain infrastructure, and regulate pricing. When utilities fail to perform effectively, the entire energy system suffers, leading to outages, inefficiencies, or rising costs.

Why It Matters

Middle actors are the glue that holds systems together. When they perform well, they enable efficiency, coordination, and resilience. But if they become bottlenecks or misuse their influence, they can disrupt the system's flow. Understanding their role allows you to optimize these critical connections and improve overall performance.

For instance, in a workplace, a manager who effectively coordinates between executives and employees ensures clear communication and smooth operations. Conversely, a manager who withholds information or creates unnecessary bureaucracy can slow progress and frustrate team members.

1. **Identify Middle Actors:** Choose a system you interact with, such as a supply chain or a project team. Visualize the intermediaries and consider how they impact the system's flow.

2. **Analyze a Bottleneck:** Think of a middle actor who slows down the system. What causes the bottleneck, and how could it be addressed?

3. **Redesign a Middle Actor's Role:** For a system you're part of, propose ways to optimize the role of an intermediary. Could they take on new responsibilities or use better tools?

Key Takeaway

Middle actors link and shape systems — grasping their role enables you to enhance their impact and boost system performance.

Chapter 38: See Intermediary Goals

The Balancing Act

Intermediaries within a system often serve as bridges between different components, but they aren't neutral players. They have their own goals, which might align with, complement, or conflict with the system's overall objectives. Recognizing these intermediary goals is critical for understanding how systems operate and where friction or inefficiencies may arise.

For instance, in a supply chain, a logistics company may aim to maximize profit, while the retailer it serves prioritizes cost reduction. If their goals aren't aligned, the logistics company might cut corners on delivery quality, creating dissatisfaction for the retailer's customers.

Intermediary goals often influence how resources are allocated, how decisions are made, and how effectively the system functions. By understanding these goals, you can address conflicts, build alignment, and improve system-wide outcomes.

How to See Intermediary Goals

1. **Identify the Intermediaries:** Map the system and locate the players who connect different parts, such as managers, contractors, or distributors.

2. **Understand Their Objectives:** Ask what these intermediaries aim to achieve. Are their goals purely financial, or do they include other priorities like efficiency, reputation, or growth?

3. **Assess Goal Alignment:** Compare the intermediary's goals with the system's overall objectives. Are they working toward the same outcomes, or are their priorities misaligned?

4. **Monitor Trade-offs:** Intermediaries often balance competing demands. Consider whether their decisions create value for the entire system or just for their own role.

Real-World Example

In financial systems, investment brokers act as intermediaries between investors and markets. While their goal is to facilitate trades, they might also prioritize earning commissions, leading to conflicts of interest. This misalignment can result in brokers recommending frequent trades that benefit them but harm their clients' portfolios.

Why It Matters

Intermediary goals shape how systems function. Misaligned goals can create inefficiencies, conflicts, or poor outcomes, while well-aligned goals foster collaboration and system-wide success. Recognizing and addressing these dynamics ensures that intermediaries contribute to, rather than detract from, the system's objectives.

For example, in a non-profit organization, aligning the goals of fundraisers (securing donations) with program teams (delivering impact) ensures that resources are allocated effectively and mission objectives are met.

Exercises

1. **Identify Intermediary Goals:** Choose an intermediary in a system you know, such as a manager or contractor. Reflect on their goals and how they align with the broader system.

2. **Analyze a Conflict:** Think of a situation where intermediary goals created friction. How did this affect the system, and what changes could improve alignment?

3. **Propose a Realignment:** For a misaligned intermediary in a system you interact with, brainstorm ways to align their goals with the system's overall objectives.

Key Takeaway

Intermediaries have their own goals — understanding and aligning these goals with the system's objectives creates smoother, more effective operations.

Chapter 39: Spot the Pace of Change

Why Speed Matters

Systems don't change at a uniform pace. Some evolve rapidly, driven by innovation, crises, or competition, while others shift slowly due to entrenched norms, resource constraints, or bureaucratic inertia. The pace of change in a system significantly affects its outcomes, adaptability, and long-term stability. Recognizing the speed at which a system operates allows you to anticipate challenges, plan interventions, and ensure the system's evolution aligns with its goals.

For example, the technology industry moves quickly, with constant innovations reshaping markets and consumer behavior. In contrast, public education systems often evolve slowly, requiring years to implement new policies or teaching methods. Each pace has its pros and cons: rapid change can foster innovation but risks instability, while slow change allows for careful deliberation but may struggle to adapt to urgent needs.

By spotting the pace of change, you can align your actions with the system's natural rhythm or introduce mechanisms to accelerate or decelerate its evolution as needed.

How to Spot the Pace of Change

1. **Observe the System's History:** Study past changes to understand how quickly the system has evolved over time. Does it adapt frequently, or are shifts rare and significant?

2. **Analyze External Pressures:** Systems often respond to external forces like market demands, technological advances, or societal expectations. Faster systems are often subject to intense competition or innovation, while slower systems may operate in stable or regulated environments.

3. **Identify Internal Constraints:** Look for structural factors that limit the pace of change, such as rigid hierarchies, resource shortages, or deeply embedded traditions.

4. **Assess Feedback Loops:** Rapid systems tend to have tight, short-term feedback loops, while slower systems may rely on longer cycles of evaluation and response.

Real-World Example

Consider urban planning. Large infrastructure projects like building highways or public transit systems often unfold over decades due to funding challenges, political debates, and community involvement. In contrast, temporary solutions like bike lanes or ride-sharing services can emerge quickly, addressing immediate transportation needs while larger projects progress.

Why It Matters

The pace of change determines how effectively a system can respond to opportunities or challenges. Ignoring the system's speed risks misaligned strategies — pushing too fast may lead to instability, while moving too slowly can result in missed opportunities.

For instance, a business trying to implement a fast-paced digital transformation in a traditionally slow-moving organization may face resistance and burnout. Conversely, a company that waits too long to adapt to industry changes risks losing market relevance. Aligning with the system's natural pace — or strategically modifying it — ensures smoother, more effective transitions.

Exercises

1. **Analyze a System's Speed:** Choose a system you interact with, such as your workplace or a local community project. Reflect on whether it changes quickly or slowly and why.

2. **Plan a Change Strategy:** For a system with a defined pace of change, brainstorm how you might align your goals with its rhythm. For example, should you accelerate or slow down your efforts?

3. **Simulate a Different Pace:** Imagine speeding up or slowing down a system's change process. What benefits and risks would this create?

Key Takeaway:

Systems evolve at different speeds — recognizing their pace of change allows you to align strategies and ensure sustainable evolution.

Chapter 40: Detect Systemic Fragility

The Weakness of Rigidity

Fragile systems are those that cannot adapt to stress or disruption. Unlike resilient systems, which bend and recover, fragile systems break when faced with unexpected challenges. Detecting systemic fragility allows you to identify vulnerabilities and build strategies to make the system more robust and adaptable.

Fragility often arises from rigidity — overly strict rules, reliance on single points of failure, or excessive focus on efficiency at the expense of flexibility. For instance, a company that relies on one supplier for critical materials is fragile; any disruption to that supplier can halt operations. Similarly, a financial system optimized for short-term gains but unprepared for economic shocks can collapse during crises.

Fragility isn't always obvious. Systems may appear stable under normal conditions, only to fail dramatically when faced with sudden changes. Detecting these vulnerabilities before they cause failure is essential for long-term sustainability.

How to Detect Systemic Fragility

1. **Look for Single Points of Failure:** Identify components that, if disrupted, would collapse the entire system. Examples include sole suppliers, critical infrastructure, or over-reliance on specific individuals.
2. **Evaluate Adaptability:** Test whether the system can adjust to changing conditions. Rigid systems often resist adaptation, leading to fragility.
3. **Analyze Stress Scenarios:** Consider how the system would respond to extreme events, such as economic downturns, natural disasters, or sudden market shifts.
4. **Watch for Over-Optimization:** Systems focused solely on efficiency often lack the redundancy or slack needed to handle disruptions.

Real-World Example

The COVID-19 pandemic exposed fragility in global supply chains. Many industries relied on "just-in-time" manufacturing, which minimized inventory to cut costs. When production disruptions occurred, these supply chains collapsed, leaving companies unable to meet demand. Introducing redundancies — such as multiple suppliers or inventory buffers — could have mitigated this fragility.

Why It Matters

Fragile systems are prone to catastrophic failure, often without warning. By detecting fragility early, you can redesign systems to handle stress, adapt to change, and recover from disruptions. Resilient systems aren't just stronger—they're also more sustainable and better equipped to seize opportunities in uncertain environments.

For example, a community with diverse sources of energy — solar, wind, and backup generators—is more resilient than one relying solely on a centralized power grid. Similarly, a workplace that cross-trains employees ensures continuity if key team members are unavailable.

Exercises

1. **Identify a Single Point of Failure:** Think of a system you interact with, such as a workflow or a household routine. Pinpoint a dependency that could disrupt the entire system if it fails.

2. **Analyze a Past Disruption:** Reflect on a time when a system you relied on failed. What made it fragile, and how could it have been strengthened?

3. **Design for Resilience:** Choose a system and propose ways to make it less fragile, such as adding redundancies, increasing flexibility, or planning for disruptions.

Key Takeaway

Fragile systems break under stress — detecting vulnerabilities early allows you to build resilience and ensure long-term stability.

Part 3: Spotting Patterns in Natural Systems

Natural systems are rich with lessons for understanding complexity. From the rhythmic cycles of seasons to the dynamic flow of energy through ecosystems, nature provides a blueprint for how interconnected systems operate. These systems evolve, adapt, and self-correct in ways that humans often overlook but can learn from to design better solutions. This section explores the recurring patterns, interactions, and adaptations that make natural systems resilient and sustainable. By recognizing these patterns, you can apply their principles to solve problems, optimize designs, and build systems that thrive in harmony with their environment.

Chapter 41: See Cycles Everywhere

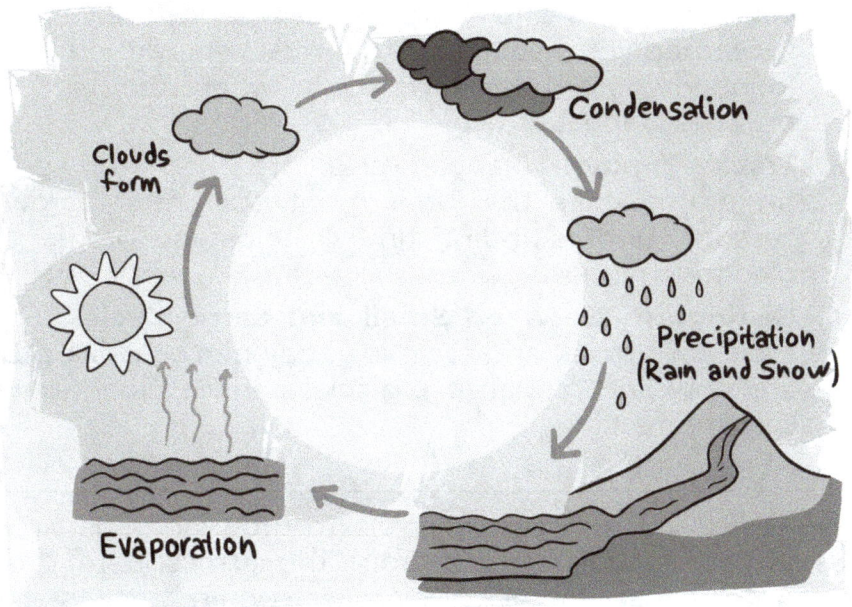

The Rhythm of Nature

Cycles are one of the most defining features of natural systems. They are the recurring processes that shape ecosystems, regulate resources, and sustain life. From the orbit of planets creating seasons to the daily rise and fall of tides, cycles bring predictability and balance to nature's complexity.

Consider the water cycle. Rain falls, fills rivers, and eventually evaporates, returning to the atmosphere. This cycle ensures that water — a finite resource — is continuously redistributed and made available to support life. Similarly, seasonal cycles dictate when animals migrate, plants flower, and farmers plant crops. Without these predictable rhythms, life would struggle to adapt and thrive.

Recognizing cycles allows you to anticipate changes, manage resources wisely, and align your actions with the system's natural rhythm.

How to Spot Cycles

1. **Look for Repetition:** Observe processes or behaviors that occur repeatedly over time, such as migrations, breeding seasons, or nutrient renewal.

2. **Outline Inputs and Outputs:** Cycles often involve the movement of resources (e.g. water, energy, nutrients). Identify where these flows begin, where they end, and how they repeat.

3. **Track Timing:** Many cycles are tied to specific timeframes, like the lunar month or annual growing seasons. Understanding timing helps you predict and plan for changes.

4. **Distinguish Between Small and Large Cycles:** Some cycles are quick and local (e.g. day-night), while others are slow and global (e.g. glacial periods). Identify how they interact.

Real-World Example

Forests rely on the carbon cycle to grow and sustain life. Trees absorb carbon dioxide from the atmosphere during photosynthesis, storing it as biomass. When trees die and decompose, this carbon returns to the soil or the air, completing the cycle. Interrupting this rhythm — such as through deforestation — can disrupt entire ecosystems and contribute to climate change.

Why It Matters

Understanding cycles helps you manage resources sustainably and predict system behavior. For example, farmers who align planting schedules with seasonal cycles maximize crop yields while conserving water and soil health. Similarly, businesses that anticipate economic cycles can make smarter decisions about expansion or investment.

Ignoring cycles, on the other hand, risks inefficiency, waste, or disaster. For instance, overharvesting during a population's reproductive cycle can lead to species collapse, disrupting the broader ecosystem.

Exercises

1. **Identify Cycles in Your Life:** Reflect on cycles you rely on, such as meal preparation, work schedules, or sleep patterns. How do these rhythms affect your daily life?

2. **Observe a Natural Cycle:** Spend time observing a natural process, like the phases of the moon or the growth of a plant. Reflect on how it repeats and supports other systems.

3. **Map a System's Cycle:** Choose a system you interact with (e.g. water usage or food production). Visualize its inputs, outputs, and how they repeat over time.

Key Takeaway

Cycles bring rhythm and balance to systems. Recognizing and aligning with them creates harmony and sustainability.

Chapter 42: Understand Energy Flows

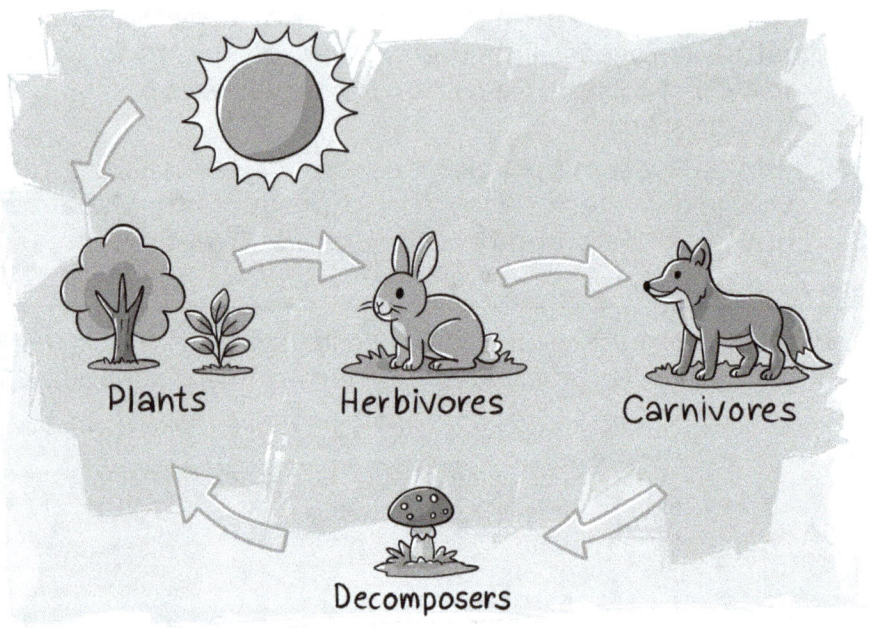

Plants   Herbivores   Carnivores

Decomposers

The Currency of Life

Energy is the driving force of all natural systems. It flows from one part of an ecosystem to another, enabling growth, movement, reproduction, and renewal. Understanding energy flows reveals how systems function, where inefficiencies arise, and how to optimize processes.

In most ecosystems, the sun is the primary energy source. Plants capture solar energy through photosynthesis, converting it into food that fuels other organisms. Herbivores consume plants, transferring energy to the next level of the food chain, while predators continue the flow. Decomposers, like fungi and bacteria, break down dead organisms, returning energy and nutrients to the soil. This cycle ensures that energy flows continuously through the system, sustaining life.

How to Understand Energy Flows

1. **Follow the Energy Source:** Identify the primary energy input (e.g. sunlight, food, fuel) and trace how it moves through the system.

2. **Track Transformations:** Energy changes form as it flows—solar energy becomes chemical energy in plants, which becomes kinetic energy in animals. Map these transformations.

3. **Identify Losses:** No system is perfectly efficient. Look for where energy is lost (e.g. as heat or waste) and consider how these losses affect the system.

4. **Observe Recursive Patterns:** Some energy flows create self-perpetuating cycles, such as a population explosion of herbivores leading to overgrazing and ecosystem collapse.

Real-World Example

In agriculture, energy flows directly impact productivity. Crops capture solar energy, which humans and livestock consume. Excessive tilling or overuse of fertilizers can disrupt this flow, depleting soil energy and reducing long-term yields. Sustainable practices like crop rotation or organic farming help maintain energy balance.

Why It Matters

Energy flows determine the efficiency and resilience of a system. Systems that manage energy poorly — whether through waste, overuse, or misallocation — become unsustainable and prone to failure. Understanding energy flows allows you to optimize processes, reduce inefficiencies, and design systems that last.

For instance, renewable energy systems like solar or wind power mimic natural energy flows, harnessing and converting energy sustainably. Businesses or cities that adopt these systems reduce reliance on finite resources while maintaining energy security.

Exercises

1. **Trace Energy in Your Life:** Consider how energy flows through your daily routine. What fuels your food, transportation, or electricity use?

2. **Visualize an Ecosystem's Energy Flow:** Choose an ecosystem (e.g. a garden or forest) and outline how energy flows between its components. Reflect on where energy is gained or lost.

3. **Optimize an Energy System:** Identify an energy flow you rely on, like home heating or food storage. Brainstorm ways to reduce waste or increase efficiency.

Key Takeaway

Energy flows are the lifeblood of natural systems. Tracking and optimizing them ensures sustainability and efficiency.

Chapter 43: Uncover Predator-Prey Dynamics

The Balance of Nature

Predator-prey dynamics are one of the most fascinating and critical aspects of natural systems. These relationships shape ecosystems by regulating populations, controlling resources, and maintaining balance. Predators keep prey populations in check, preventing overgrazing or resource depletion, while prey availability determines predator survival.

For instance, wolves in Yellowstone National Park play a vital role in controlling deer and elk populations. Without wolves, these herbivores overgraze vegetation, leading to ecosystem degradation. Reintroducing wolves restored balance, allowing plant life to recover, which in turn benefited birds, insects, and even rivers that were less impacted by erosion.

Predator-prey dynamics are not just about direct interactions. They ripple throughout ecosystems. A single predator's actions can affect everything from vegetation growth to the behavior of other species. Understanding these dynamics reveals the interconnectedness of natural systems and the importance of every component.

How to Uncover Predator-Prey Dynamics

1. **Identify the Players:** Start by mapping the predators and prey within the system. What species interact, and how do their populations fluctuate?

2. **Analyze Population Cycles:** Predator and prey populations often rise and fall in cycles, with one influencing the other. Look for patterns over time.

3. **Observe Ripple Effects:** Predator-prey dynamics extend beyond direct relationships. How do changes in these populations affect plants, competitors, or other species?

4. **Consider Human Influence:** Humans often disrupt predator-prey dynamics through activities like hunting, farming, or habitat destruction. Assess how these changes impact the broader system.

Real-World Example

Shark populations in marine ecosystems regulate fish species. Overfishing of sharks can lead to a boom in mid-level predators, which then overconsume smaller fish or marine plants, destabilizing the entire food web. Protecting sharks restores this balance, ensuring the health of coral reefs and other marine ecosystems.

Why It Matters

Predator-prey dynamics highlight the balance required for ecosystems to thrive. Disrupting these relationships—such as removing predators or overexploiting prey—can lead to cascading failures that destabilize entire systems. Recognizing and respecting these dynamics is essential for conservation, resource management, and ecosystem restoration.

For example, when humans hunt top predators to near extinction, it often creates unintended consequences, like the spread of invasive species or crop destruction by unchecked herbivores. Protecting these predators preserves the equilibrium and health of the broader system.

Exercises

1. **Define a Predator-Prey Relationship:** Choose an ecosystem (e.g. a forest or ocean) and map its predator-prey dynamics. Reflect on how these interactions shape the environment.

2. **Analyze Human Impact:** Think of a predator-prey system affected by human activity, such as urban expansion or fishing. What changes have occurred, and how could they be addressed?

3. **Simulate a Disruption:** Imagine removing a predator or prey species from a system you've studied. Predict how this would affect the ecosystem's balance.

Key Takeaway

Predator-prey dynamics regulate ecosystems. Understanding these relationships ensures balance and prevents cascading failures.

Chapter 44: Trace Nutrient Paths

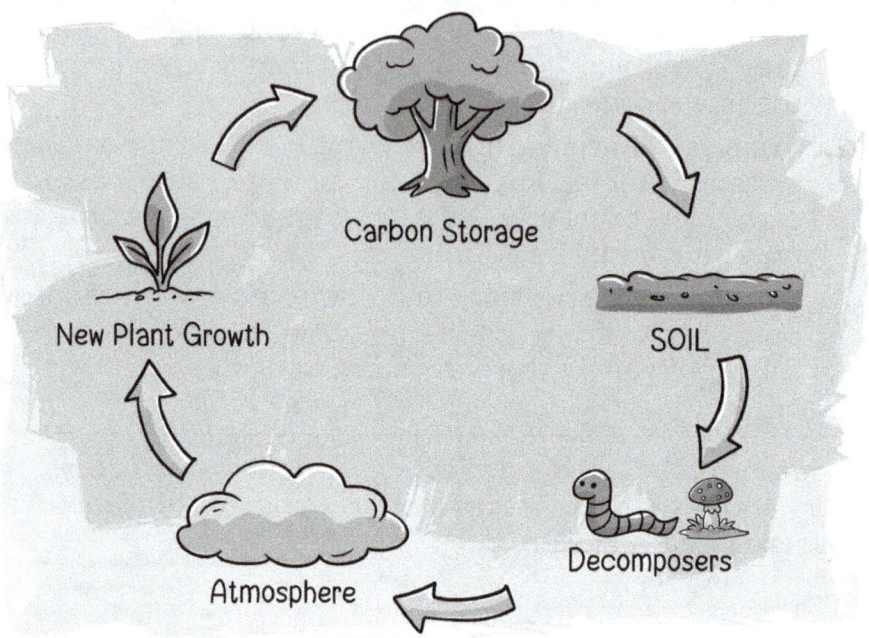

Carbon Storage

New Plant Growth

SOIL

Decomposers

Atmosphere

The Circulation of Life's Building Blocks

Nutrients like carbon, nitrogen, and phosphorus move through ecosystems in complex but predictable pathways. These nutrient cycles sustain life by ensuring essential elements are continually recycled and made available to living organisms. Understanding these paths allows you to see how ecosystems maintain balance and where disruptions can cause systemic problems.

For instance, in the carbon cycle, plants absorb carbon dioxide from the atmosphere during photosynthesis, storing it in their tissues. When plants die, decomposers break down the organic material, releasing carbon back into the soil and air. This continuous flow supports life while maintaining the planet's carbon balance.

Nutrient paths don't just sustain individual species — they link entire ecosystems. When one part of the cycle is disrupted, such as through excessive carbon emissions or deforestation, the ripple effects can destabilize the system.

How to Trace Nutrient Paths

1. **Identify the Elements:** Focus on one nutrient, like nitrogen or phosphorus. Where does it come from, and how does it move through the system?

2. **Trace the Flow:** Create a diagram showing how the nutrient cycles between the atmosphere, soil, plants, animals, and decomposers.

3. **Look for Bottlenecks:** Disruptions in nutrient paths — like soil depletion or pollution — can create bottlenecks that limit the system's efficiency.

4. **Consider External Inputs:** Human activities like agriculture or industry often introduce excess nutrients, causing imbalances like algal blooms or soil degradation.

Real-World Example

The nitrogen cycle is essential for agriculture, but excessive fertilizer use disrupts it. Runoff from farms introduces excess nitrogen into rivers, causing algal blooms that deplete oxygen and harm aquatic life. Sustainable farming practices, like crop rotation and controlled fertilizer use, help restore balance.

Why It Matters

Tracing nutrient paths reveals how ecosystems sustain life and adapt to change. Ignoring these cycles leads to inefficiencies, waste, or even ecological collapse. For example, deforestation interrupts the water and carbon cycles, reducing soil fertility and accelerating climate change. Restoring these cycles improves ecosystem health and resilience.

Understanding nutrient paths also provides insights for sustainable practices. Composting, for instance, mimics natural nutrient recycling, turning organic waste into valuable resources that enrich the soil and reduce landfill waste.

Exercises

1. **Map a Nutrient Cycle:** Choose a nutrient like carbon or phosphorus and sketch out its flow through a local ecosystem. Reflect on how it supports life.

2. **Identify a Disruption:** Think of a nutrient cycle affected by human activity (e.g. industrial emissions or deforestation). How has this disruption impacted the ecosystem?

3. **Design a Restoration Plan:** Propose ways to restore balance to a disrupted nutrient cycle, such as reforestation, composting, or reducing pollution.

Key Takeaway

Nutrient paths sustain ecosystems. Tracing these cycles reveals opportunities to restore balance and improve sustainability.

Chapter 45: Find Anchor Points

The Pillars of Stability

Anchor points are the critical species, processes, or elements that hold ecosystems together. Without them, the entire system can collapse or become unbalanced. These elements often have a disproportionate impact relative to their size or visibility, making them essential for the system's health and resilience.

For example, consider coral reefs. Though they occupy less than 1% of the ocean floor, they support approximately 25% of all marine species by providing habitat, food, and shelter. Coral itself acts as an anchor point for the reef ecosystem — without healthy coral, the entire network of species it supports would decline.

Anchor points aren't always obvious. They can range from a keystone species like wolves in Yellowstone to physical elements like soil in a forest. Identifying these critical components allows you to focus conservation or intervention efforts where they matter most.

1. **Identify Disproportionate Impacts:** Look for species or elements that have an outsized effect on the system compared to their size or population. For instance, a small predator might regulate prey populations that would otherwise overconsume resources.

2. **Observe System Dependencies:** Analyze which parts of the system rely heavily on a specific element or species. This might include plants that provide the primary food source for herbivores or water sources that sustain entire ecosystems.

3. **Monitor Changes:** Pay attention to what happens when an element is removed or disrupted. A significant system-wide response often indicates an anchor point.

4. **Consider Indirect Effects:** Anchor points often stabilize systems indirectly, such as by maintaining a balance between competing species or supporting key nutrient flows.

Real-World Example

In tropical rainforests, large fruit-bearing trees are anchor points that sustain biodiversity. These trees provide food for a wide range of animals, from insects to birds to larger mammals like monkeys. When these trees are cut down, the ripple effects disrupt food availability, pollination, and habitat, destabilizing the entire ecosystem.

Why It Matters

Anchor points are the foundation of ecosystem stability. Protecting them ensures the long-term health and resilience of the system, while ignoring or removing them can lead to cascading failures. For instance, overfishing keystone species like sharks or tuna can destabilize entire marine food webs, allowing smaller prey populations to explode and overconsume resources.

By identifying anchor points, you can target conservation and resource management efforts more effectively. For example, protecting pollinators like bees helps stabilize agricultural systems, ensuring food security and biodiversity.

1. **Identify Anchor Points in an Ecosystem:** Choose an ecosystem you know (e.g. a local park or a coral reef). Identify one or two anchor points and reflect on how they stabilize the system.

2. **Analyze a Loss of Stability:** Think of a time when an anchor point in a system you know was disrupted (e.g. a tree being cut down or a species going extinct). What were the ripple effects?

3. **Develop a Protection Strategy:** For a critical anchor point you've identified, brainstorm ways to protect or restore it. This might include replanting trees, regulating fishing, or reducing pollution.

Key Takeaway

Anchor points are essential for stability. Protecting them prevents system collapse and ensures resilience.

Chapter 46: Notice Niche Functions

The Specialists of Nature

In every ecosystem, species or processes perform unique roles that contribute to the system's overall success. These are called niche functions, and they often fill critical gaps that other elements cannot. Without them, the system may lose balance, become less efficient, or struggle to recover from disruptions.

Consider dung beetles, which may seem unimportant at first glance. Their niche function involves breaking down animal waste, recycling nutrients back into the soil, and reducing parasites. Without dung beetles, ecosystems would struggle with waste accumulation, nutrient depletion, and disease outbreaks.

Niche functions aren't limited to species. They can include unique processes, like the way fungi decompose dead material and make nutrients available to plants. Recognizing and valuing these roles allows you to appreciate how every part of an ecosystem contributes to its overall health.

How to Notice Niche Functions

1. **Look for Specialists:** Identify species or processes that perform highly specific roles, such as certain insects that pollinate only one type of flower.

2. **Trace Dependencies:** Consider what other parts of the system rely on this function. For instance, a plant that depends on a specific pollinator is an indicator of a niche relationship.

3. **Observe Redundancy or Lack of It:** Some niche functions are irreplaceable, while others may have backups. For example, multiple species might perform similar roles in diverse ecosystems, increasing resilience.

4. **Monitor System Disruptions:** Niche functions often become apparent when they're missing — what happens if a specific species disappears?

Real-World Example

In forests, woodpeckers perform a niche function by creating cavities in trees that later serve as nesting sites for birds, bats, and insects. If woodpeckers are absent, species that depend on these cavities struggle to find shelter, reducing biodiversity and ecosystem resilience.

Why It Matters

Niche functions ensure that ecosystems operate efficiently and adapt to change. Losing these functions can create bottlenecks or gaps that weaken the system. For example, the decline of a pollinator species can disrupt entire food webs, affecting crops, wild plants, and the animals that depend on them.

Protecting niche functions is often a cost-effective way to maintain ecosystem health. For instance, promoting the conservation of soil microbes improves nutrient cycling, reducing the need for chemical fertilizers and enhancing agricultural productivity.

Exercises

1. **Identify a Niche Function:** Think of a specific species or process in a system you know (e.g. a scavenger or a decomposer). Reflect on its unique role and how it supports the ecosystem.

2. **Observe Dependencies:** Choose an ecosystem and identify which parts depend on a specific niche function. How would its loss affect the system?

3. **Propose a Protection Plan:** For a niche function you've identified, brainstorm ways to safeguard or enhance it, such as habitat preservation or species reintroduction.

Key Takeaway

Niche functions are vital for ecosystem efficiency. Recognizing and protecting them ensures that systems remain balanced and resilient.

Chapter 47: Evaluate Mechanisms

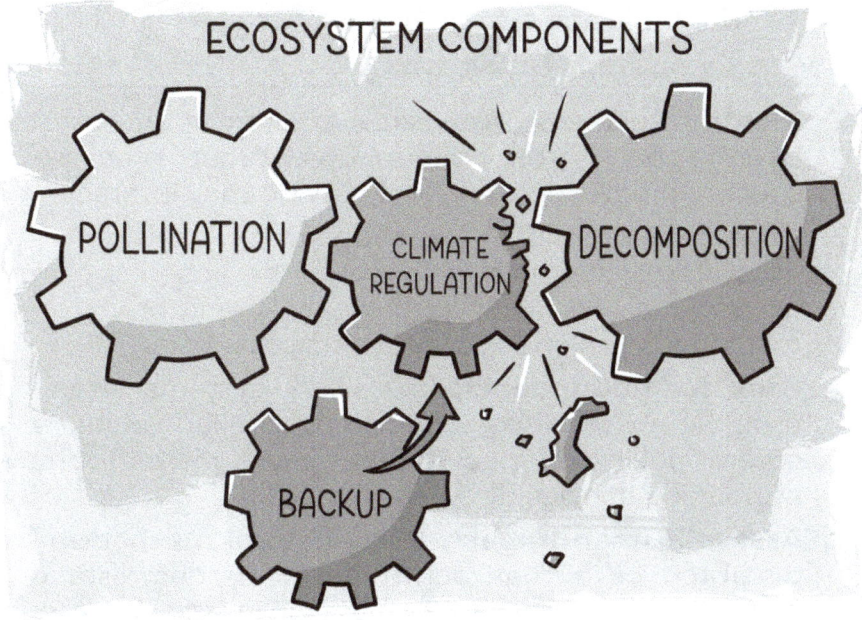

ECOSYSTEM COMPONENTS

POLLINATION

CLIMATE REGULATION

DECOMPOSITION

BACKUP

Nature's Tools for Resilience

Ecosystems are remarkably adept at recovering from disruptions, whether it's a forest regrowing after a wildfire or a river cleansing itself after pollution. These recovery processes depend on mechanisms—natural tools and processes that allow systems to restore balance, adapt, and thrive. By evaluating these mechanisms, you can better understand what makes ecosystems resilient and how to support their recovery when stressed.

For example, after a volcanic eruption devastates a landscape, pioneer species like mosses and lichens play a crucial role in recolonizing the area. These species prepare the environment for more complex plants, gradually rebuilding the ecosystem over time. This mechanism of ecological succession ensures that life can bounce back, even after severe disruptions.

Evaluating mechanisms involves looking at both how ecosystems respond to stress and how they maintain equilibrium under normal conditions. Understanding these tools not only reveals the inner workings of natural systems but also offers valuable lessons for designing human systems that are more adaptable and sustainable.

How to Evaluate Mechanisms

1. **Identify Recovery Processes:** Look at how ecosystems bounce back from disruptions. What processes or species initiate recovery, and how do they interact?

2. **Analyze Stability Mechanisms:** Consider how ecosystems maintain balance in the absence of major disruptions. For example, what keeps predator-prey relationships in check or prevents soil erosion?

3. **Look for Redundancies:** Resilient systems often have multiple mechanisms performing similar functions, like several pollinator species that ensure plants reproduce even if one species declines.

4. **Assess Human Impact:** Many natural mechanisms are disrupted by human activity, such as deforestation or pollution. Evaluate how these impacts weaken the system's ability to recover.

Real-World Example

Wetlands act as natural water filtration mechanisms, trapping pollutants and sediments while maintaining water quality. When wetlands are destroyed for development, this mechanism is lost, leading to water contamination and increased flood risks. Restoring wetlands reactivates this natural tool, improving both ecosystem and human resilience.

Why It Matters

Mechanisms are the building blocks of resilience. Without them, ecosystems become fragile and less capable of adapting to stress. By evaluating these processes, you can identify where systems are vulnerable and how to strengthen them.

For instance, rewilding initiatives, which reintroduce species like wolves or beavers, aim to restore lost mechanisms that stabilize ecosystems. Beavers, for example, create dams that regulate water flow, prevent flooding, and create habitats for other species. These mechanisms benefit not just the ecosystem but also human communities nearby.

Exercises

1. **Observe a Recovery Mechanism:** Spend time in a natural area that has experienced disruption (e.g. a burned forest or a polluted river). Note how the ecosystem is recovering and which processes are involved.

2. **Map Stability Mechanisms:** Choose an ecosystem and identify the mechanisms that maintain its balance, such as nutrient cycling or predator-prey dynamics.

3. **Propose a Restoration Plan:** For a disrupted ecosystem, brainstorm ways to restore its natural mechanisms, like reintroducing species or reducing human impact.

Key Takeaway

Natural mechanisms drive resilience. Evaluating them helps you understand how ecosystems recover and how to support their stability.

Chapter 48: Find Cascading Effects

The Domino Effect in Ecosystems

Ecosystems are networks of interdependent relationships, where changes in one part can trigger a series of effects throughout the system. These cascading effects can amplify problems or create unexpected consequences, often far removed from the initial change. Recognizing these ripple effects is essential for understanding how ecosystems respond to disturbances and how to predict long-term impacts.

For example, when sea otter populations decline, sea urchins — one of their main prey — can proliferate unchecked. These urchins overgraze kelp forests, reducing habitat for fish and other marine life. This single disruption affects not only biodiversity but also fisheries that depend on healthy kelp ecosystems.

Cascading effects aren't always negative. Reintroducing wolves to Yellowstone National Park reduced deer overpopulation, allowing vegetation to recover and stabilizing riverbanks. Understanding these effects reveals how small interventions can create significant and sometimes surprising outcomes.

How to Find Cascading Effects

1. **Map Interdependencies:** Identify the connections between species, resources, and processes within the ecosystem. Look for elements that influence multiple others.

2. **Trace the Initial Change:** Examine what caused the initial disturbance, such as the removal of a predator or the introduction of an invasive species.

3. **Follow the Ripple Effects:** Analyze how the change impacts other components, both directly and indirectly. These effects often move through multiple levels of the system.

4. **Anticipate Long-Term Outcomes:** Cascading effects can take time to fully manifest. Consider how current changes might evolve and influence future conditions.

Real-World Example

The introduction of non-native zebra mussels into freshwater ecosystems is a classic example of cascading effects. These mussels filter plankton from the water, reducing food availability for native species and altering nutrient cycles. Their proliferation can also clog water intake systems, creating economic costs for humans.

Why It Matters

Cascading effects demonstrate the interconnectedness of ecosystems. Ignoring these ripple effects can lead to unintended consequences, like resource depletion or ecosystem collapse. Recognizing them allows for more informed decisions and interventions that account for both immediate and long-term impacts.

For example, in agriculture, excessive pesticide use may control pests initially but can also harm pollinators, reduce soil health, and create resistance in pest populations. Understanding these cascades helps farmers adopt practices like integrated pest management that minimize negative outcomes.

Exercises

1. **Sketch a Cascade:** Choose an ecosystem change (e.g. deforestation or overfishing) and map its direct and indirect effects on the system.

2. **Analyze a Positive Cascade:** Reflect on a time when a small intervention created widespread benefits, such as planting native vegetation to restore habitats.

3. **Design a Controlled Intervention:** For a system you know, propose an intervention and predict its cascading effects. Consider both positive and negative outcomes.

Key Takeaway

Cascading effects reveal how interconnected systems are. Understanding them helps you predict outcomes and design smarter interventions.

Chapter 49: Detect Resource Competition

The Struggle for Survival

In natural systems, resources like water, sunlight, nutrients, and space are finite. When multiple organisms or groups depend on the same limited resource, competition arises. This competition shapes how ecosystems evolve, which species thrive, and which ones decline. Detecting resource competition is essential for understanding the dynamics of any system, as it reveals where tensions exist and where interventions might stabilize the balance.

For example, in forests, tall trees compete for sunlight by growing higher, shading out smaller plants that cannot reach the canopy. In grasslands, plants with extensive root systems compete for water, often leaving shallow-rooted species at a disadvantage during droughts. These competitive interactions determine the structure, diversity, and resilience of ecosystems.

Resource competition doesn't just happen between species. It can also occur within a single population, as individuals compete for mates, food, or territory. Understanding these dynamics sheds light on how ecosystems self-regulate and how external factors, such as human activity, can disrupt this balance.

How to Detect Resource Competition

1. **Identify Shared Resources:** Determine which resources (e.g. water, sunlight, nutrients) are critical to the organisms or groups in the system.

2. **Observe Overlaps:** Look for instances where multiple species or groups depend on the same resource. Are there visible signs of competition, like slower growth or reduced diversity?

3. **Analyze Outcomes:** Study which species or groups are thriving and which are struggling. Competition often results in winners and losers, with weaker competitors being displaced or eliminated.

4. **Monitor External Pressures:** Human activities like deforestation or overfishing often intensify resource competition, pushing ecosystems beyond their limits.

Real-World Example

Overfishing in marine ecosystems creates intense resource competition among remaining species. For instance, when large fish are removed from a food web, smaller species may compete aggressively for the same prey, leading to imbalances and declines in biodiversity. This overexploitation also forces human communities dependent on fishing into direct competition for dwindling resources.

Why It Matters

Resource competition is a driving force in shaping ecosystems. It determines which species coexist, which adapt, and which disappear. Detecting these dynamics helps you understand why systems behave the way they do and what changes might tip the balance.

For instance, in agriculture, understanding resource competition between crops and weeds allows farmers to manage fields more effectively, minimizing losses without over-relying on chemical solutions. Similarly, urban planners can study competition for space and resources to design cities that reduce stress on natural and human systems.

Ignoring resource competition can lead to overexploitation, system collapse, or conflict. By recognizing these tensions early, you can design interventions that reduce competition and promote coexistence, such as restoring degraded habitats or redistributing resources.

Exercises

1. **Map Resource Competition:** Choose an ecosystem (e.g. a forest or ocean) and identify which species compete for critical resources. Reflect on how this competition shapes the ecosystem.

2. **Analyze Human Impact:** Think of a system where human activity has intensified resource competition, such as water use in agriculture. What consequences have emerged, and how could they be mitigated?

3. **Propose a Coexistence Strategy:** For a competitive system you've studied, brainstorm ways to reduce conflict and promote resource sharing, such as introducing buffer zones or optimizing resource use.

Key Takeaway

Resource competition shapes ecosystems. Detecting and managing it ensures balance, biodiversity, and long-term sustainability.

Chapter 50: Observe Natural "Evolution"

ADAPTATION OVER TIME

Adapting to Survive

Evolution is nature's way of adapting to change. Over generations, species develop traits that help them survive and thrive in their environments. This process, driven by natural selection, shapes ecosystems, determines biodiversity, and creates systems that are dynamic and resilient. Observing natural evolution provides insight into how systems respond to pressures, adapt to new conditions, and maintain balance over time.

For instance, the beaks of Darwin's finches evolved to suit the types of food available on their islands. On islands with hard seeds, finches developed stronger, thicker beaks. On islands with flowers, their beaks became longer and more delicate to reach nectar. These adaptations illustrate how species evolve to fill ecological niches and maintain the system's diversity.

Natural evolution isn't limited to biology. Processes like rivers carving landscapes or plants adapting to urban environments also demonstrate how systems evolve in response to change. Recognizing these shifts helps you understand how systems self-correct and find new equilibrium points.

How to Observe Natural Evolution

1. **Identify Adaptations:** Look for traits in organisms or systems that seem uniquely suited to their environments. What pressures might have driven these adaptations?

2. **Trace Changes Over Time:** Study how species or systems have evolved in response to environmental changes. Are there visible shifts in behavior, structure, or function?

3. **Look for Unintended Consequences:** Evolution often produces trade-offs, where adaptations benefit survival in one way but create vulnerabilities in others.

4. **Consider External Influences:** Human activity can accelerate or disrupt natural evolution, as seen in antibiotic resistance or urban wildlife adapting to new environments.

Real-World Example

Peppered moths in industrial England evolved darker coloration to blend into soot-covered trees, avoiding predation. When pollution was reduced, lighter-colored moths regained dominance, showing how evolution reflects environmental conditions.

Why It Matters

Observing natural evolution reveals how systems adapt and innovate in response to challenges. This understanding is vital for managing ecosystems, predicting future changes, and designing human systems that mimic nature's adaptability.

For example, sustainable agriculture draws inspiration from evolution by developing crops resistant to drought or pests, reducing reliance on chemical interventions. Similarly, urban planners can study how plants and animals adapt to city life, using this knowledge to design greener, more resilient spaces.

Ignoring evolutionary processes can lead to unintended consequences. For instance, overusing pesticides accelerates the evolution of resistant pests, creating new challenges for farmers. Understanding and working with natural evolution helps systems stay balanced and sustainable.

Exercises

1. **Identify an Evolutionary Trait:** Choose a species or system and identify one of its adaptations. Reflect on how this trait benefits its survival and any trade-offs it creates.

2. **Trace Evolutionary Change:** Study a species or system that has visibly evolved over time (e.g. antibiotic resistance or urban wildlife). What pressures drove this change?

3. **Apply Evolutionary Lessons:** For a challenge in your life or work, think of ways to mimic evolutionary processes. How can you adapt to changes and build resilience?

Key Takeaway

Evolution is nature's way of adapting to change. Observing these processes reveals how systems innovate, balance, and thrive over time.

Chapter 51: Recognize Interconnected Ecosystems

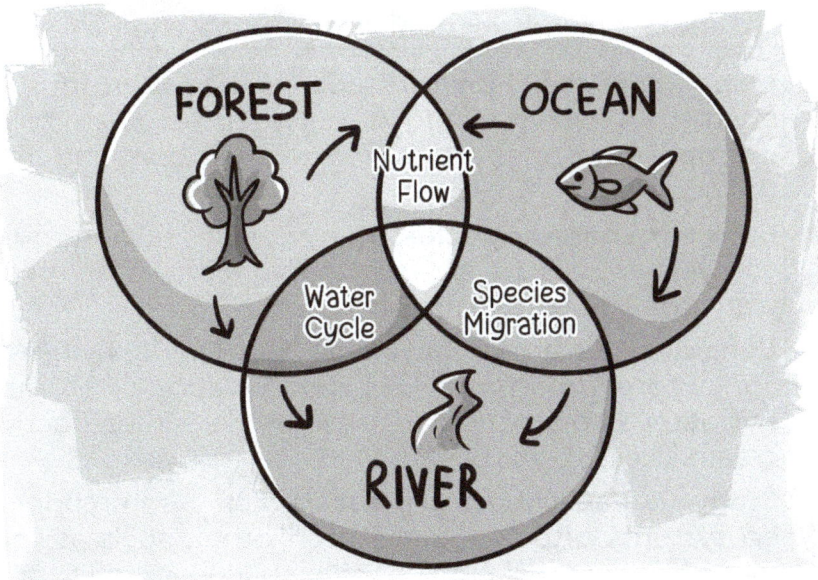

Nothing Exists in Isolation

Ecosystems are not isolated entities. They're part of a larger network of interconnected systems that influence and depend on one another. What happens in one ecosystem often ripples into others, creating a web of interactions that sustain life on Earth. Recognizing these interconnections allows you to see the broader picture, where changes in one system can have cascading effects on others.

For example, forests play a critical role in regulating the water cycle by absorbing rainfall and releasing moisture into the atmosphere. This process influences nearby rivers, which depend on consistent water flow, and even oceans, where the rivers eventually drain. Similarly, nutrients washed from forests into rivers provide food for aquatic life, which in turn supports marine ecosystems. Disrupting one part of this chain — such as by deforesting a watershed—can destabilize the entire network.

Interconnected ecosystems teach us an essential lesson: everything is connected. By understanding these links, you can predict and mitigate unintended consequences, fostering a more holistic approach to conservation and resource management.

How to Recognize Interconnected Ecosystems

1. **Map Resource Flows:** Trace how water, nutrients, energy, or species move between ecosystems. For example, how does a river connect a mountain forest to the ocean?

2. **Look for Shared Species:** Many species rely on multiple ecosystems, such as migratory birds that nest in wetlands and feed in forests.

3. **Consider External Impacts:** Human activities like agriculture, urbanization, or deforestation often disrupt ecosystem connections. Identify where these activities create stress.

4. **Study Ecosystem Feedbacks:** Interconnected ecosystems often regulate each other, such as forests influencing rainfall patterns that sustain agriculture.

Real-World Example

Mangrove forests are a vital connection point between land and sea. They stabilize coastlines, filter pollutants from rivers, and provide nurseries for fish species that support both marine ecosystems and local fisheries. When mangroves are removed for development, these benefits are lost, leading to erosion, declining fish populations, and degraded water quality downstream.

Why It Matters

Recognizing interconnected ecosystems helps you see the full picture of how natural systems sustain life. Ignoring these links can lead to decisions that solve problems in one area but create new ones elsewhere. For instance, diverting rivers for irrigation might boost crop yields in the short term but deplete water supplies for downstream communities and ecosystems.

By understanding these connections, you can design solutions that benefit multiple ecosystems simultaneously. For example, restoring wetlands not only improves local biodiversity but also filters water, reduces flooding, and supports neighboring ecosystems like rivers and oceans.

Exercises

1. **Trace an Ecosystem Connection:** Choose two ecosystems near you, such as a forest and a river. Define how they influence and depend on each other.

2. **Analyze a Human Impact:** Think of a human activity, like farming or deforestation, that affects multiple ecosystems. What are the ripple effects, and how could they be mitigated?

3. **Design a Holistic Solution:** For a problem affecting one ecosystem, brainstorm ways to address it without harming connected systems. Could your solution benefit multiple ecosystems?

Key Takeaway

Ecosystems are deeply interconnected. Recognizing these links allows you to design solutions that support the health of entire networks.

Chapter 52: Spot Self-Healing Solutions

Nature's Built-In Repairs

Nature is a master of resilience. Many ecosystems have built-in mechanisms that allow them to heal themselves after disruptions, from storms to human intervention. These self-healing solutions rely on natural processes like regrowth, nutrient cycling, and species reintroduction to restore balance and functionality. Recognizing and supporting these processes can lead to sustainable, low-cost solutions for environmental challenges.

For instance, prairies and grasslands are adapted to recover from wildfires. Fire clears dead vegetation, releases nutrients into the soil, and encourages the growth of fire-resistant plants. Rather than preventing all fires, allowing controlled burns can activate these self-healing processes, improving the ecosystem's health.

How to Spot Self-Healing Solutions

1. **Identify Resilient Species:** Look for plants, animals, or processes that thrive in disrupted environments. These often play key roles in recovery.

2. **Observe Natural Recovery:** Study how ecosystems bounce back after disturbances like storms, droughts, or fires. What processes drive this recovery?

3. **Minimize Interference:** Self-healing processes often require minimal human intervention. Consider whether your actions support or hinder these natural mechanisms.

4. **Analyze Ecosystem Design:** Ecosystems with diverse species and redundant processes are often better equipped for self-healing.

Real-World Example

Coral reefs can recover from bleaching events if water conditions improve and stressors like overfishing or pollution are reduced. Left undisturbed, resilient coral species repopulate the reef, rebuilding habitats for marine life. Protecting reefs through marine reserves and pollution control gives these self-healing mechanisms a chance to work.

Why It Matters

Self-healing solutions are efficient, sustainable, and often require fewer resources than human interventions. Ignoring these processes can lead to unnecessary costs and disruptions, while working with them enhances recovery and resilience.

For example, reforesting degraded land with native plants supports self-healing by encouraging soil regeneration, water retention, and biodiversity recovery. In contrast, planting non-native species might slow these processes and create new challenges.

Understanding self-healing solutions also helps us design systems that mimic nature. Green infrastructure projects, like rain gardens, replicate natural water filtration processes, reducing the need for costly artificial solutions.

Exercises

1. **Observe Natural Recovery:** Visit an area recovering from disruption, like a cleared field or burned forest. Note the signs of self-healing, such as plant regrowth or animal return.

2. **Support a Self-Healing Process:** Think of a system you interact with that could recover naturally, like a garden or pond. How can you minimize interference and support its recovery?

3. **Design a Self-Healing System:** Apply the concept to a human system, like a workplace or community project. How could you build in processes that allow it to recover from setbacks?

Key Takeaway

Nature is inherently resilient. Spotting and supporting self-healing solutions ensures efficient, sustainable recovery from disruptions.

Chapter 53: See Nature's Redundancies

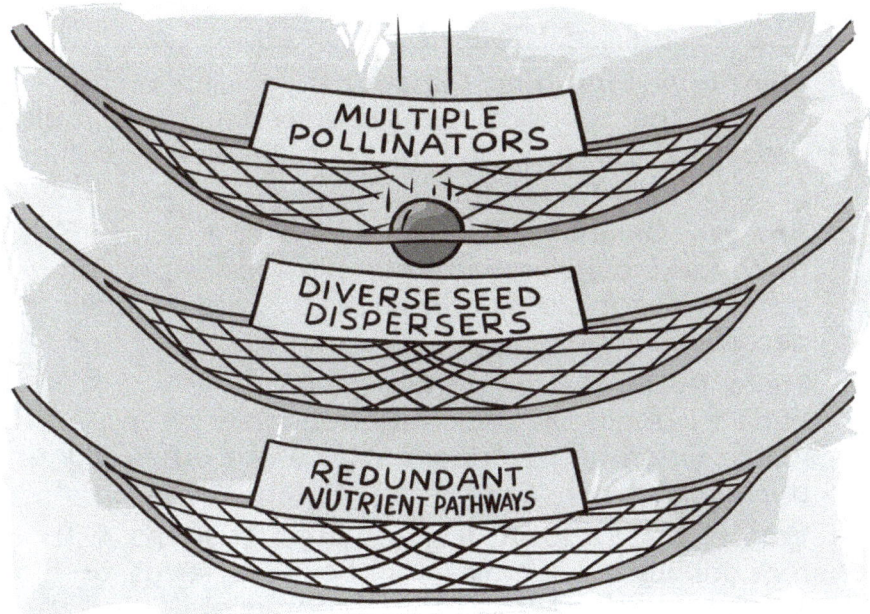

Built-In Backups for Survival

Redundancy is nature's way of ensuring resilience. In ecosystems, multiple species or processes often perform the same function, providing backups when one element is disrupted. This redundancy allows systems to maintain stability even under stress, ensuring continuity despite challenges like environmental changes or species loss.

For instance, tropical rainforests have numerous species of pollinators — bees, bats, birds, and butterflies — all contributing to the reproduction of plants. If one pollinator species declines due to disease or habitat loss, others can step in, preventing widespread disruption to the ecosystem. This overlap of functions creates a buffer that helps ecosystems adapt and thrive.

Seeing nature's redundancies highlights the importance of diversity. While efficiency may seem appealing, systems that rely too heavily on a single species, resource, or process become fragile and vulnerable to collapse. Nature shows us that redundancy is not waste, it's insurance.

How to See Nature's Redundancies

1. **Identify Overlapping Functions:** Look for processes or species that perform similar roles, such as multiple predators controlling prey populations or different plants stabilizing soil.

2. **Analyze Diversity:** Diverse ecosystems tend to have more redundancies, with multiple species providing the same ecosystem services (e.g. pollination, decomposition).

3. **Trace Responses to Stress:** Observe how the system behaves under disruption. Redundancy often becomes visible when one component fails but others continue the function.

4. **Watch for Lack of Redundancy:** Systems with low redundancy — such as monoculture farms or highly specialized industries — are more fragile.

Real-World Example

Mangroves provide multiple layers of redundancy in coastal protection. They reduce storm surges, trap sediment, and stabilize shorelines. If one mangrove species declines, others can perform similar roles, ensuring continued protection for coastal ecosystems and human communities. In contrast, engineered solutions like seawalls lack this redundancy and fail if damaged.

Why It Matters

Redundancy is critical for resilience. Systems that lack backups are prone to failure when their single point of reliance breaks down. For example, monoculture farming, which relies on one crop species, is vulnerable to pests or diseases, while polyculture farming creates redundancy by incorporating multiple crops that support each other.

Recognizing nature's redundancies also helps inform better system design. From urban planning to supply chains, building in overlapping functions ensures flexibility and adaptability. For example, decentralized energy grids with multiple renewable sources mimic the resilience of ecosystems, reducing the risk of widespread blackouts.

Exercises

1. **Spot Redundancies in Nature:** Choose an ecosystem (e.g. a forest or wetland) and identify overlapping functions or species that provide backups. Reflect on how these redundancies improve resilience.

2. **Analyze a Fragile System:** Think of a human system that lacks redundancy, such as a single-source supply chain or an over-reliance on one service. What risks does this create?

3. **Design for Redundancy:** Apply nature's principle of redundancy to a project or system you're part of. How can you build in backups to ensure continuity under stress?

Key Takeaway

Nature's redundancies ensure resilience. Incorporating overlapping functions in systems reduces fragility and prepares them for disruptions.

Chapter 54: Trace Habitat Fragmentation

Breaking the Web of Life

Habitat fragmentation occurs when large, continuous ecosystems are broken into smaller, disconnected patches. This fragmentation disrupts species movement, reduces biodiversity, and makes ecosystems less resilient to change. Tracing habitat fragmentation reveals how human activities like deforestation, road construction, and urban sprawl impact natural systems — and what can be done to restore connectivity.

For example, when forests are cleared for agriculture, wildlife corridors are severed, preventing species from migrating to find food, mates, or shelter. Over time, isolated populations become genetically weaker, reducing their ability to adapt to environmental changes. Fragmentation also impacts ecological processes like pollination and seed dispersal, as the animals responsible for these tasks can no longer move freely.

Understanding habitat fragmentation helps you see the bigger picture of ecosystem health. It highlights the need for strategies like wildlife corridors, reforestation, and land-use planning to restore connections and support biodiversity.

How to Trace Habitat Fragmentation

1. **Map Ecosystem Breaks:** Identify areas where natural habitats have been divided by roads, farmland, or urbanization. Focus on regions where connectivity is essential for wildlife.

2. **Analyze Impacts on Movement:** Study how fragmentation affects species' ability to move. Are populations becoming isolated, or are migration patterns disrupted?

3. **Look for Edge Effects:** Fragmentation creates edges— areas where habitat meets human-altered land. These edges often have different conditions, such as increased light or invasive species, which can harm native ecosystems.

4. **Assess Long-Term Risks:** Consider how fragmentation affects ecosystem resilience. Are species more vulnerable to extinction, or are ecosystems losing key functions like pollination?

Real-World Example

The Amazon rainforest is heavily fragmented by logging and agriculture, creating isolated patches of forest. This limits the movement of species like jaguars and toucans, disrupting food webs and reducing genetic diversity. Efforts to reconnect these fragments through wildlife corridors and protected reserves are critical for restoring balance.

Why It Matters

Habitat fragmentation weakens ecosystems by reducing biodiversity, disrupting ecological processes, and increasing vulnerability to climate change. Left unchecked, it can lead to species extinction and collapse of vital ecosystem services.

Tracing fragmentation highlights opportunities for restoration. For instance, reconnecting fragmented forests with wildlife corridors allows species to move freely, restoring migration patterns and genetic diversity. Similarly, urban green spaces and rooftop gardens create pockets of habitat in cities, supporting pollinators and other wildlife.

Exercises

1. **Outline Fragmentation Near You:** Choose a natural area and identify how human development has fragmented the habitat. Reflect on how this impacts species and ecosystem health.

2. **Analyze Edge Effects:** Visit a fragmented habitat and observe the edges. How do they differ from the interior, and how might they affect native species?

3. **Propose a Connectivity Plan:** For a fragmented system, brainstorm ways to restore connections, such as wildlife corridors, reforestation, or changes in land-use policies.

Key Takeaway

Habitat fragmentation disrupts ecosystems. Tracing and addressing these breaks restores connectivity and supports biodiversity.

Chapter 55: Watch Energy Minimization Strategies

The Efficiency of Nature

In natural systems, energy is a limited resource, and organisms have evolved strategies to use it as efficiently as possible. Energy minimization strategies allow species to conserve resources, reduce effort, and maximize survival. From the way birds fly in formation to the way plants grow toward sunlight, nature constantly finds ways to do more with less.

For example, geese flying in a V-formation take advantage of aerodynamic efficiency. The lead bird works hardest, creating a slipstream that reduces air resistance for the trailing birds. As the lead bird tires, another bird takes its place, ensuring the flock can travel long distances without exhausting any one member. This cooperative energy-sharing strategy exemplifies nature's focus on efficiency.

By watching these energy-saving methods, you can uncover lessons for designing human systems that optimize resource use and minimize waste. These principles apply everywhere — from engineering to team management to sustainable agriculture.

How to Watch Energy Minimization Strategies

1. **Observe Natural Movements:** Study how animals move in groups, like fish schools or bird flocks, to identify cooperative strategies that save energy.

2. **Track Resource Allocation:** Look for how organisms prioritize energy use, such as plants directing resources toward growth in sunlight-rich areas.

3. **Analyze Adaptations:** Many adaptations, like streamlined shapes in aquatic animals or hibernation in mammals, are designed to reduce energy expenditure.

4. **Find Examples in Human Systems:** Notice where energy minimization strategies already appear in human systems, such as shared transportation or optimized workflows.

Real-World Example

Ant colonies exemplify energy efficiency. Worker ants divide tasks like foraging, building, and defending the colony to minimize overlap and maximize productivity. Pheromone trails direct ants to the most efficient routes, ensuring that resources like food are gathered quickly and with minimal energy waste.

Why It Matters

Energy minimization strategies create resilience by allowing organisms and systems to thrive with limited resources. Ignoring these strategies can lead to inefficiency, waste, and unsustainable practices. For instance, industries that fail to optimize energy use may incur higher costs and environmental impacts.

By learning from nature, you can design systems that mimic these strategies. For example, businesses can adopt energy-efficient logistics, such as grouping deliveries to reduce fuel consumption. Similarly, urban planners can design cities that minimize commuting distances, reducing energy use for transportation.

Recognizing energy minimization also helps identify areas for improvement in existing systems. If a workflow or ecosystem is expending unnecessary energy, redesigning it with efficiency in mind can lead to better outcomes with fewer resources.

Exercises

1. **Observe Natural Efficiency:** Choose a natural process (e.g. animal migration or plant growth) and identify how energy is minimized. Reflect on what makes the process efficient.

2. **Analyze Human Efficiency:** Think of a system you interact with, like transportation or food production. Where is energy wasted, and how could it be conserved?

3. **Design an Energy-Saving System:** Apply an energy minimization strategy you've observed in nature to a human system, such as a workplace or community project.

Key Takeaway

Nature thrives by minimizing energy use. Observing these strategies can inspire more efficient and sustainable human systems.

Chapter 56: Look for Mutualism

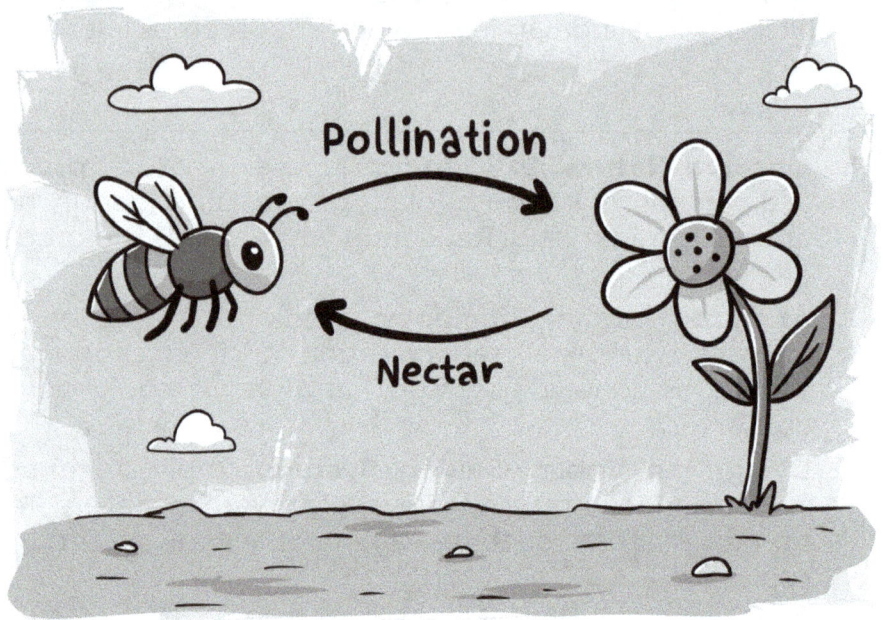

Win-Win Relationships

Mutualism is one of nature's most fascinating strategies for success. It occurs when two or more species interact in ways that benefit all parties involved. These win-win relationships enhance survival, efficiency, and resilience, creating partnerships that strengthen entire ecosystems.

Consider bees and flowering plants. Bees collect nectar to feed their colonies, while flowers rely on bees to transfer pollen, enabling reproduction. This mutualistic relationship ensures the survival of both species and benefits broader systems like agriculture and biodiversity.

Mutualism isn't limited to species — it can involve entire ecosystems working together. For example, coral reefs host diverse marine species that depend on each other for shelter, food, and protection. Recognizing mutualism reveals how cooperation, not just competition, drives natural systems.

How to Look for Mutualism

1. **Identify Interactions:** Observe species that regularly interact, such as plants and pollinators or predators and scavengers. Consider how both parties benefit.

2. **Trace Dependencies:** Study how these relationships impact the broader system. For example, how does pollination benefit not just plants but also herbivores and predators?

3. **Observe Human-Nature Mutualism:** Look for ways humans benefit from and support ecosystems, such as through sustainable farming practices.

4. **Note Breakdowns:** Mutualism can fail under stress, such as when habitat loss disrupts pollinator-plant relationships. Analyze how to restore these partnerships.

Real-World Example

Sea anemones and clownfish have a classic mutualistic relationship. Clownfish live among anemone tentacles for protection from predators, while the anemone benefits from the clownfish removing debris and deterring potential threats. This partnership enhances survival for both species.

Why It Matters

Mutualism highlights the power of cooperation. Systems that foster mutual benefit are more resilient, sustainable, and efficient than those driven solely by competition. Ignoring mutualism can lead to imbalances, such as declines in crop yields when pollinator populations drop.

Understanding mutualism also inspires human systems. For example, partnerships between businesses and communities — such as companies supporting local farmers — create shared benefits that promote long-term success. Similarly, urban green spaces foster mutualism by improving residents' quality of life while supporting biodiversity.

Recognizing and supporting mutualistic relationships ensures stability and sustainability. When mutualism thrives, so does the system.

Exercises

1. **Identify a Mutualistic Pair:** Choose a species pair (e.g. bees and flowers) and reflect on how their relationship benefits both. How does this partnership impact the broader system?

2. **Analyze a Mutualism Breakdown:** Think of a mutualistic relationship disrupted by human activity (e.g. habitat loss or pollution). How might it be restored?

3. **Design a Mutualistic System:** Apply mutualism to a human system, such as a workplace or community. How can cooperation create shared benefits?

Key Takeaway

Mutualism drives resilience in nature. Fostering win-win relationships builds stronger, more sustainable systems.

Chapter 57: Detect Adaptive Behaviors

The Power of Flexibility

Adaptation is the hallmark of resilience in natural systems. Ecosystems and species continually adjust their behaviors, structures, or functions in response to changes in their environment. These adaptive behaviors help maintain balance, survive disruptions, and evolve over time. Detecting adaptive behaviors reveals how systems respond to stress and offers clues for designing systems that thrive in dynamic conditions.

For example, desert plants like cacti adapt to arid conditions by storing water in their tissues and developing spines to minimize evaporation. Similarly, animals like Arctic foxes change their fur color with the seasons — white in winter for camouflage in snow and brown in summer to blend with the tundra. These adaptations allow species to succeed in challenging and changing environments.

Understanding adaptive behaviors isn't just about marveling at nature's ingenuity — it's about learning from it. Observing these behaviors provides insights into how human systems can become more flexible, innovative, and sustainable.

How to Detect Adaptive Behaviors

1. **Observe Changes Over Time:** Look for shifts in how species or systems behave in response to environmental changes, such as migration patterns or feeding habits.

2. **Analyze Behavioral Triggers:** Identify what factors prompt adaptive behaviors, such as resource scarcity, predators, or climate fluctuations.

3. **Look for Structural Changes:** Adaptation isn't always about behavior—sometimes it involves physical changes, like thicker fur or deeper roots.

4. **Trace Feedback Cycles:** Adaptive behaviors often arise from dynamic interconnections in systems, where stress or disruption prompts self-correction.

Real-World Example

Coral reefs adapt to water conditions by building structures that support symbiotic relationships with algae. However, when water temperatures rise, corals expel algae in a process called bleaching, an adaptive behavior aimed at surviving stress. If conditions improve, the algae return, restoring the reef's balance.

Why It Matters

Adaptive behaviors are essential for survival and resilience. Systems that fail to adapt risk collapse when conditions change, while those that adjust can thrive in the face of uncertainty. For example, businesses that adapt to market trends—like shifting to online sales during a pandemic—are more likely to succeed than those that resist change.

Detecting adaptive behaviors in natural systems also inspires solutions for human challenges. Urban planners can learn from floodplain ecosystems that adapt to seasonal changes, designing cities that flex with water levels instead of resisting them. Similarly, organizations can adopt adaptive leadership models that respond dynamically to challenges.

Understanding adaptation allows you to anticipate change and design systems that align with it, rather than working against it.

Exercises

1. **Observe Adaptive Behavior:** Choose a species or ecosystem and identify how it adjusts to environmental changes, such as seasonal shifts or resource scarcity.

2. **Analyze a Human System:** Think of a system (e.g. a workplace or community) that successfully adapted to a challenge. What made this adaptation effective?

3. **Design an Adaptive System:** Apply principles of adaptation to a project or goal you're working on. How can you build flexibility into the system to handle future changes?

Key Takeaway

Adaptive behaviors help systems thrive in changing conditions. Detecting and learning from them builds resilience and flexibility in human systems.

Chapter 58: Understand Biotic-Abiotic Interactions

Where Life Meets the Elements

Ecosystems are shaped by interactions between living (biotic) and non-living (abiotic) components. Plants, animals, fungi, and microbes rely on water, sunlight, air, and soil to survive, while these abiotic factors are in turn influenced by the activities of organisms. Understanding these interactions reveals how ecosystems function, adapt, and evolve.

For example, plants absorb sunlight and carbon dioxide to produce energy through photosynthesis, creating oxygen as a by-product. This oxygen supports animals and microbes, which in turn produce carbon dioxide through respiration, completing a cycle that balances gases in the atmosphere. Abiotic factors like temperature and precipitation also regulate where certain plants and animals can thrive, shaping biodiversity in different regions.

Recognizing biotic-abiotic interactions highlights the deep interconnectedness of life and environment. It shows how changes in one domain — such as pollution or deforestation — can ripple across both living organisms and non-living systems.

How to Understand Biotic-Abiotic Interactions

1. **Map Resource Flows:** Trace how abiotic resources like sunlight, water, and nutrients move through a system and support biotic components.
2. **Identify Feedback Mechanisms:** Look for cycles where living organisms influence abiotic factors, such as plants regulating soil nutrients or animals aerating the soil.
3. **Observe Environmental Limits:** Analyze how abiotic factors like temperature or pH set boundaries for where species can survive.
4. **Consider Disruptions:** Study how human activities like pollution or urbanization alter biotic-abiotic relationships, creating imbalances.

Real-World Example

Mangroves demonstrate the profound interplay between biotic and abiotic factors. Their roots stabilize soil, reducing erosion, while also filtering saltwater and improving water quality. In turn, this abiotic support enables a rich ecosystem of fish, birds, and other species to thrive. When mangroves are destroyed, these interactions collapse, leading to habitat loss and water degradation.

Why It Matters

Biotic-abiotic interactions are the foundation of ecosystem health. Ignoring these relationships can lead to environmental degradation, resource scarcity, and biodiversity loss. For example, over-extraction of water (an abiotic resource) for agriculture can dry up wetlands, disrupting the habitats of countless species.

Understanding these interactions also informs sustainable practices. For instance, farmers who maintain healthy soil biota (biotic) improve nutrient cycling and water retention (abiotic), boosting crop yields while reducing the need for chemical inputs. Similarly, urban designers can use green infrastructure to harmonize biotic and abiotic systems, like planting trees to regulate urban temperatures.

Exercises

1. **Map an Interaction:** Choose a local ecosystem and trace one biotic-abiotic interaction, such as how plants influence soil quality or how water availability affects animal populations.

2. **Analyze a Disruption:** Think of a system where human activity has disrupted biotic-abiotic interactions (e.g. deforestation or mining). What are the consequences, and how could they be mitigated?

3. **Propose a Balance:** Design a project or practice that restores harmony between biotic and abiotic factors, such as reforestation to improve water quality.

Key Takeaway

Biotic-abiotic interactions sustain ecosystems. Recognizing these connections promotes stronger environmental stewardship and smarter system design.

Chapter 59: See Human-Nature Interactions

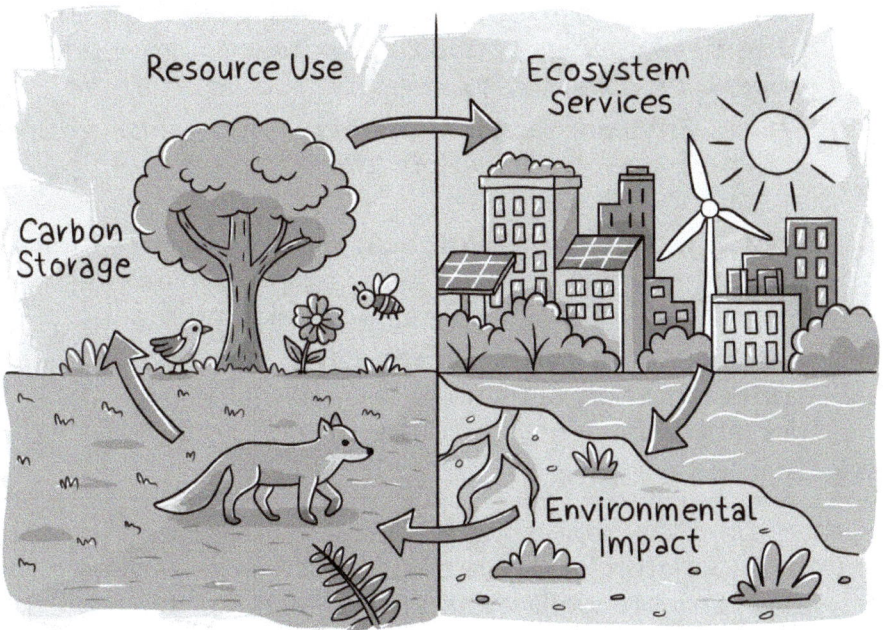

A Two-Way Relationship

Humans and nature are deeply intertwined, each shaping the other over time. Human activities, from farming to urbanization, impact natural systems, while ecosystems provide essential resources and services that sustain human life. Recognizing these interactions helps uncover both the benefits humans derive from nature and the challenges they impose on it.

For example, forests act as carbon sinks, absorbing carbon dioxide and regulating the climate — services that benefit human health and agriculture. In return, deforestation disrupts these functions, contributing to climate change and reducing biodiversity. This two-way relationship underscores the need for balance.

By understanding these interactions, you can identify opportunities to align human activities with natural processes, fostering sustainable coexistence rather than conflict.

How to See Human-Nature Interactions

1. **Map Resource Dependencies:** Identify how human systems — such as agriculture, water supply, or energy— depend on natural resources and ecosystem services.

2. **Trace Environmental Impacts:** Study how human activities like construction, transportation, or industry affect natural systems.

3. **Look for Positive Feedback:** Observe where humans actively support nature, such as through reforestation, habitat restoration, or sustainable farming practices.

4. **Assess Long-Term Trade-Offs:** Evaluate whether current human activities are sustainable or if they risk depleting the ecosystems they depend on.

Real-World Example

Urban gardens represent a positive interaction between humans and nature. They provide fresh food, reduce urban heat, and support pollinators like bees and butterflies. In return, humans tend to these spaces, ensuring their health and productivity while reconnecting with the natural world.

Why It Matters

Human-nature interactions shape the planet's future. Mismanaged interactions lead to environmental degradation, resource scarcity, and declining quality of life, as seen in deforestation or pollution. Conversely, fostering harmonious interactions creates resilient systems that benefit both people and the environment.

For example, sustainable fisheries align human needs with ecological health by setting quotas and protecting breeding grounds, ensuring fish populations remain robust. Similarly, renewable energy sources like wind and solar reduce environmental impact while meeting human energy demands.

Understanding these dynamics also shifts the focus from short-term exploitation to long-term stewardship. By recognizing the mutual benefits of supporting nature, humans can create systems that thrive alongside the environment.

Exercises

1. **Map a Human-Nature Interaction:** Choose a local system, such as a park or a water source, and identify how humans use and impact it. What benefits flow in each direction?

2. **Analyze an Unsustainable Practice:** Think of a human activity that harms nature (e.g. overfishing or deforestation). What changes could make it more sustainable?

3. **Propose a Positive Interaction:** Design a project or practice that enhances human-nature interactions, like planting native species in urban areas or protecting local wetlands.

Key Takeaway

Human and natural systems are deeply connected. Recognizing these interactions creates opportunities for sustainable coexistence.

Chapter 60: Track Species Migration Networks

Highways of the Natural World

Species migration is one of nature's most dynamic and intricate processes. Birds, fish, mammals, and even insects travel vast distances, often crossing continents or oceans, to find food, reproduce, or escape changing seasons. These migration networks connect ecosystems across the globe, making them vital to biodiversity and ecosystem health.

For instance, monarch butterflies migrate thousands of miles between North America and Mexico, relying on specific habitats along the way for rest and refueling. If these habitats are disrupted — such as by deforestation or agriculture — the entire migration cycle is jeopardized, threatening the species' survival.

Tracking species migration networks reveals the interconnectedness of ecosystems and highlights the importance of preserving critical habitats along migration routes. It also underscores how changes in one location can ripple across entire regions, affecting biodiversity and ecological balance.

How to Track Species Migration Networks

1. **Identify Migratory Species:** Focus on species known for long-distance migrations, such as birds, whales, or butterflies. Study their life cycles and movement patterns.

2. **Define Critical Stopovers:** Highlight the key habitats these species rely on during migration, such as wetlands, breeding grounds, or feeding areas.

3. **Trace Threats Along Routes:** Analyze how human activities, like urbanization or climate change, disrupt these networks and what impacts result.

4. **Consider Broader Connections:** Migration networks link distant ecosystems. Study how changes in one region affect other parts of the network.

Real-World Example

The East Atlantic Flyway is a major migration route for millions of birds traveling between Europe and Africa. Along this route, wetlands like the Wadden Sea in northern Europe provide critical feeding grounds. Protecting these stopovers ensures that birds have the resources they need to complete their journeys and maintain healthy populations.

Why It Matters

Migration networks sustain ecosystems by distributing species, nutrients, and energy across regions. Disrupting these networks — such as through habitat loss or climate change — can collapse entire ecological systems and harm human communities that depend on them. For instance, the decline of migratory fish species like salmon impacts both aquatic ecosystems and the livelihoods of fishing communities.

Tracking migration networks also informs conservation efforts. By identifying and protecting key habitats, such as breeding grounds or stopover sites, you can ensure the survival of migratory species and the ecosystems they support.

Additionally, migration teaches us about adaptability and resilience. Understanding these networks inspires better design of human systems, such as transportation networks or global supply chains, to create efficient and sustainable connections.

Exercises

1. **Map a Migration Route:** Choose a migratory species and trace its route, including key habitats and stopover points. Reflect on what supports or threatens its journey.

2. **Analyze a Disrupted Network:** Think of a migration network affected by human activity, such as habitat loss or climate change. What consequences have emerged, and how could they be addressed?

3. **Design a Support Plan:** Propose ways to protect a migration network, such as creating wildlife corridors, conserving key habitats, or reducing pollution.

Key Takeaway

Migration networks connect ecosystems across the globe. Tracking and protecting these pathways ensures biodiversity and ecological balance.

Part 4: Applying Systems Thinking to Solve Problems

This final section bridges the gap between understanding systems and using that understanding to drive meaningful action. By applying systems thinking, you can tackle complex challenges, design solutions that adapt to change, and create systems that are resilient, efficient, and inclusive. From breaking problems into manageable subsystems to fostering collaboration and long-term sustainability, this section provides actionable strategies to solve real-world issues. Whether you're leading a team, managing a project, or addressing societal challenges, these tools empower you to think holistically and act decisively.

Chapter 61: Break Down the Problem into Subsystems

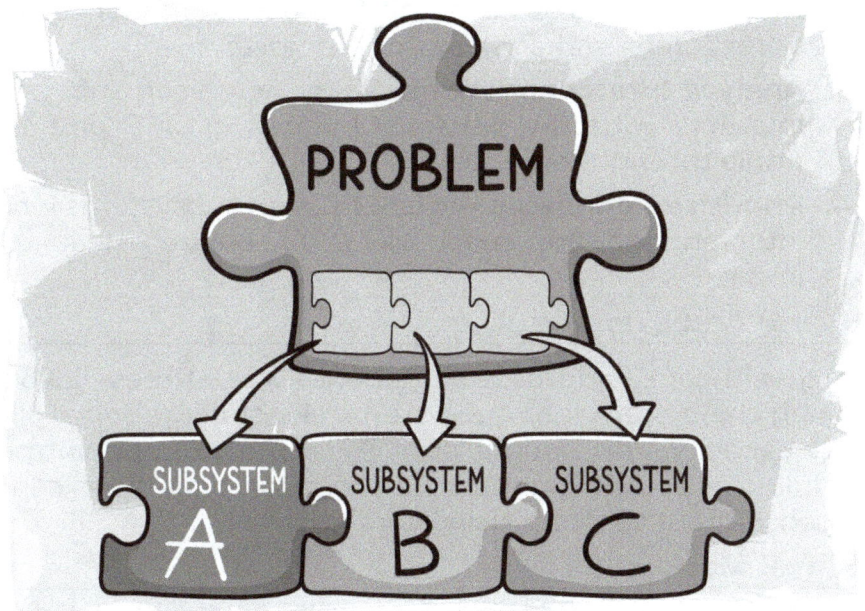

Dissecting Complexity

Large problems often feel overwhelming, but systems thinking offers a way to make them manageable: breaking them down into subsystems. These smaller, interrelated parts allow you to understand the root causes, identify connections, and develop targeted interventions without losing sight of the bigger picture.

For example, consider traffic congestion in a city. Instead of treating it as one massive issue, breaking it into subsystems— public transportation, road infrastructure, traffic laws, and driver behavior — reveals specific areas to address. Improving bus routes, optimizing traffic signals, and promoting carpooling all contribute to solving the larger problem.

This approach ensures that solutions are both effective and holistic, avoiding quick fixes that might inadvertently create new issues.

How to Break Down Problems

1. **Define the System:** Identify the overall problem and map the components that contribute to it.

2. **Isolate Subsystems:** Divide the problem into smaller, manageable parts based on function or influence, such as resources, stakeholders, or processes.

3. **Analyze Interconnections:** Study how each subsystem interacts with the others. Changes in one part may ripple through the system.

4. **Prioritize Actionable Parts:** Focus on subsystems where interventions are most likely to create meaningful impact.

Real-World Example

In healthcare, addressing patient wait times involves breaking the system into subsystems like staffing, scheduling, facility capacity, and patient flow. By improving appointment scheduling or optimizing resource allocation, wait times can be reduced without compromising care quality.

Why It Matters

Breaking down problems into subsystems makes complex challenges less intimidating and more actionable. It allows for focused, systematic interventions that address root causes rather than symptoms. For example, tackling climate change requires addressing subsystems like energy production, transportation, agriculture, and policy. Focusing solely on one aspect without considering others might lead to incomplete or counterproductive solutions.

This approach also encourages collaboration across disciplines. By identifying the components of a problem, you can involve relevant experts and stakeholders in each area, ensuring more comprehensive solutions.

Exercises

1. **Dissect a Personal Problem:** Choose a challenge you face, like time management or budgeting, and break it into subsystems. What parts can you tackle first?

2. **Analyze a Global Issue:** Select a complex issue like poverty or deforestation. Do a layout of its subsystems and think about how changes in one part might influence others.

3. **Design an Intervention:** For a subsystem you've identified, propose a targeted intervention. How would this change affect the larger system?

Key Takeaway

Breaking problems into subsystems makes them manageable and actionable. This approach ensures focused solutions without losing sight of the bigger picture.

Chapter 62: Use Feedback for Continuous Improvement

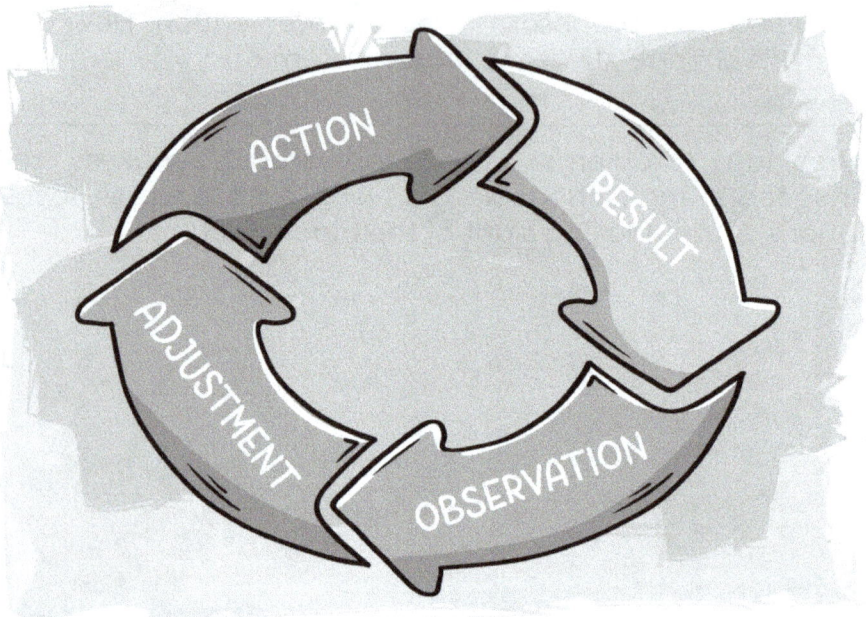

The Power of Iteration

Feedback is the cornerstone of systems thinking. By observing how actions produce results and adjusting based on what you learn, you create a continuous improvement cycle that makes systems more effective over time. Feedback allows you to identify what works, correct mistakes, and refine your approach, ensuring that solutions evolve alongside changing conditions.

For example, software development relies heavily on feedback. Developers release a product, collect user input on bugs and usability, and then update the software to better meet user needs. This iterative process ensures the product improves with each version, aligning more closely with its goals.

How to Use Feedback

1. **Set Clear Goals:** Define what success looks like so you can measure progress accurately.
2. **Collect Data:** Monitor results from actions, whether through surveys, metrics, or observations.
3. **Analyze Patterns:** Look for trends in the data that reveal what's working and what isn't.
4. **Make Adjustments:** Use what you've learned to refine your approach, and repeat the cycle for continuous improvement.

Real-World Example

In agriculture, feedback from crop yields informs farmers about the effectiveness of their practices. By testing different fertilizers or irrigation methods and monitoring results, farmers refine their strategies to maximize productivity while minimizing waste.

Why It Matters

Without feedback, systems stagnate, relying on outdated assumptions or guesswork. Continuous feedback ensures that actions remain aligned with goals, improving efficiency and effectiveness over time. For example, a company that regularly collects customer feedback can adapt its products to meet changing preferences, staying competitive in the market.

Feedback also reduces the risk of unintended consequences. By monitoring results in real-time, you can catch problems early and make course corrections before they escalate. This proactive approach saves time, money, and effort in the long run.

Exercises

1. **Apply Feedback in Your Life:** Choose a goal, like improving your diet or learning a skill. Create a feedback loop by tracking progress, reflecting on results, and adjusting your approach.
2. **Analyze a Feedback System:** Think of a system you interact with, like a workplace or school. How does it use feedback to improve? What could be done better?

3. **Design a Feedback System:** For a project or challenge, design a process that includes clear metrics, regular check-ins, and adjustment phases.

Key Takeaway

Feedback is essential for continuous improvement. Using it effectively ensures systems stay aligned with goals and adapt to changing conditions.

Chapter 63: Test Small Interventions

Why Small Steps Lead to Big Insights

When solving complex problems, starting with small, controlled interventions allows you to test ideas, observe results, and minimize risks. This approach helps uncover potential outcomes without committing significant resources or disrupting the entire system. Testing small interventions is especially valuable when working with systems that are unpredictable or have many interdependencies.

Consider urban planning. Instead of completely redesigning a city's public transit system, planners might test a single bike lane in a high-traffic area. By observing how the new lane affects traffic flow, safety, and public usage, they can refine their strategy before expanding citywide.

Small interventions act as experiments, providing insights that inform larger decisions. They reveal what works, what doesn't, and what might produce unintended consequences, making them a key tool for systems thinking.

How to Test Small Interventions

1. **Define Your Hypothesis:** Clearly state what you expect the intervention to achieve. This gives you a baseline for evaluating success or failure.

2. **Start Small:** Choose a manageable part of the system to test your idea. Look for areas where the risks are minimal but the potential insights are valuable.

3. **Observe and Measure:** Track changes carefully, using metrics or qualitative observations to understand how the system responds.

4. **Refine and Expand:** Use the results to refine your approach, then decide whether to scale the intervention or pivot to a new strategy.

Real-World Example

In public health, pilot programs are a common example of small interventions. A city might test a vaccination drive in one neighborhood before rolling it out to the entire population. By analyzing participation rates, challenges, and outcomes, officials can adjust their approach to maximize effectiveness and minimize resistance.

Why It Matters

Testing small interventions reduces risks and avoids costly mistakes. Instead of overhauling an entire system based on assumptions, you gather real-world data that informs smarter decisions. This approach also builds confidence in stakeholders, who can see tangible results before committing to larger-scale changes.

For instance, a company introducing a new product might test it in a single market before launching it globally. This trial period reveals customer reactions, potential flaws, and areas for improvement, increasing the likelihood of success at scale.

Small interventions also align with adaptive thinking. Systems are often too complex to predict all outcomes in advance, but iterative experimentation allows for ongoing learning and adjustment.

Exercises

1. **Design a Small Experiment:** Identify a problem you want to solve, such as improving a team workflow or reducing household waste. Propose a small-scale intervention to test your idea.

2. **Analyze a Past Intervention:** Think of a time when you or your organization tested a small change. What worked, what didn't, and what could have been improved?

3. **Plan a Scale-Up:** For a successful small intervention, outline the steps needed to expand it while minimizing risks.

Key Takeaway

Testing small interventions uncovers insights, minimizes risks, and builds confidence — an essential strategy for addressing complex systems.

Chapter 64: Activate Unused Resources

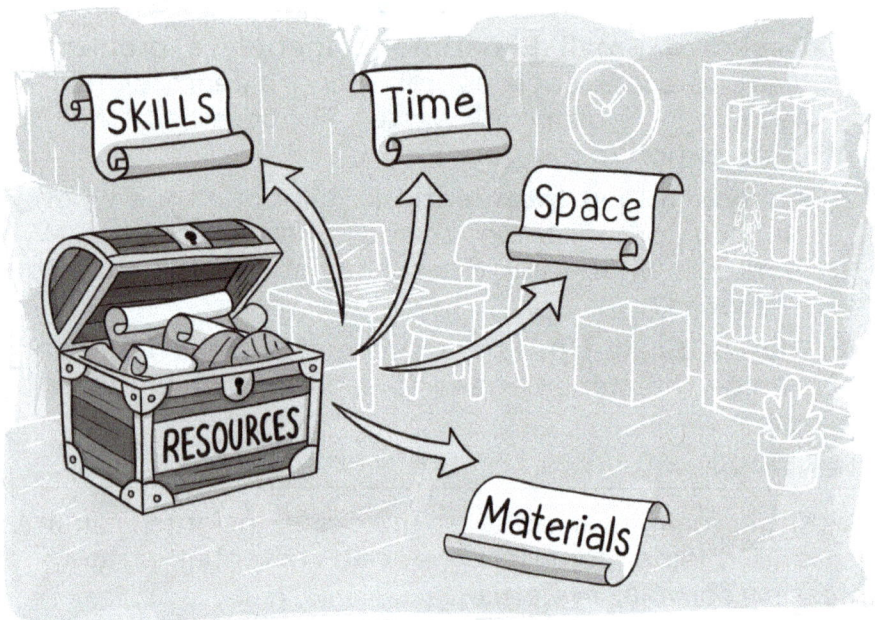

Finding the Hidden Gems in Your System

Many systems have untapped resources, whether they're underused materials, overlooked skills, or unrecognized opportunities. Activating these resources can improve efficiency, drive innovation, and unlock solutions to persistent problems. Recognizing and leveraging these hidden assets often requires a fresh perspective and creative thinking.

For example, during the COVID-19 pandemic, underutilized manufacturing facilities were retooled to produce masks, ventilators, and other critical supplies. By identifying these unused resources and repurposing them, governments and industries quickly addressed urgent needs without building new infrastructure.

Unused resources aren't always physical. They can include people's time, knowledge, or connections within a community.

Identifying and activating these assets strengthens the system as a whole.

How to Activate Unused Resources

1. **Audit the System:** Look for resources that aren't being fully utilized, such as equipment sitting idle, team members with untapped skills, or vacant spaces.

2. **Rethink Purpose:** Consider how resources could be repurposed or reallocated to add value. What new roles could they play within the system?

3. **Engage Stakeholders:** Often, those within the system are aware of overlooked resources or potential opportunities. Involve them in brainstorming solutions.

4. **Test New Uses:** Experiment with how unused resources can be applied, ensuring that the new use aligns with the system's goals.

Real-World Example

Libraries, traditionally seen as book-lending facilities, have activated unused resources to serve broader community needs. Many now provide free Internet access, meeting spaces, and job training programs, making better use of their space and infrastructure while increasing their relevance and impact.

Why It Matters

Activating unused resources is a low-cost, high-impact way to enhance system performance. It reduces waste, maximizes efficiency, and often leads to creative problem-solving. For example, businesses that repurpose leftover materials can save money while reducing environmental impact.

Unused resources are also opportunities for resilience. In times of crisis, having access to untapped assets provides flexibility and adaptability. For instance, during natural disasters, schools are often converted into emergency shelters, repurposing their space to meet urgent community needs.

Recognizing these opportunities fosters a mindset of abundance rather than scarcity. Instead of focusing on limitations, you learn to see potential in what's already available.

Exercises

1. **Identify Unused Resources:** Audit your environment — home, workplace, or community — and list resources that are underutilized. How could they be put to better use?

2. **Rethink a Current Resource:** Choose a resource you already use, such as a skill or material, and brainstorm additional ways to leverage it.

3. **Implement a New Use:** Activate one unused resource in your system. Track its impact and reflect on how it enhances efficiency or solves a problem.

Key Takeaway

Unused resources are opportunities waiting to be unlocked. Activating them strengthens systems and drives innovation.

Chapter 65: Find Nonlinear Influences

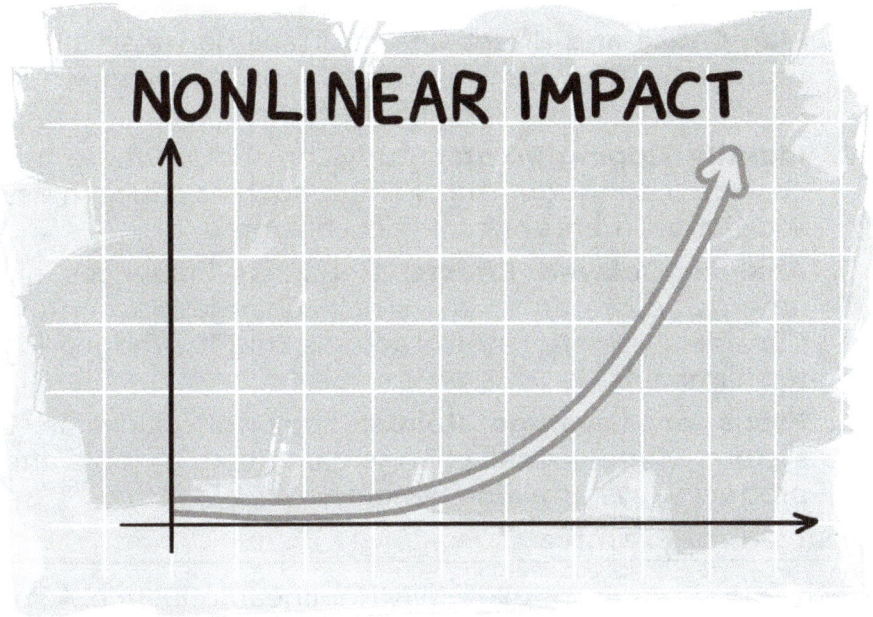

When Small Actions Create Big Waves

Not all influences in a system are proportional. Some small changes can lead to disproportionately large effects, while seemingly significant actions might barely make a dent. These nonlinear influences are critical to understanding how systems behave, and identifying them allows you to leverage small efforts for maximum impact—or prevent minor missteps from spiraling into major problems.

For example, reintroducing wolves to Yellowstone National Park is a classic case of nonlinear influence. Though the wolf population was small, their presence triggered a cascade of changes: controlling deer populations, allowing vegetation to recover, stabilizing riverbanks, and improving ecosystem health. This single intervention produced benefits far beyond its immediate scope.

Nonlinear influences often appear in tipping points, feedback cycles, or compounding effects. Finding these areas allows you to act with precision and efficiency, targeting changes that produce outsized results.

How to Find Nonlinear Influences

1. **Map Cause-and-Effect Chains:** Trace how a small input propagates through the system. Look for points where a small action creates amplified effects.

2. **Identify Tipping Points:** Study thresholds where minor changes can trigger major shifts, such as critical mass in social movements or ecological balance.

3. **Analyze Delayed Effects:** Nonlinear influences often emerge over time, as small changes accumulate. Consider how short-term actions might produce long-term impacts.

4. **Focus on Leverage Points:** Look for places in the system where a small change can create a ripple effect, producing system-wide benefits.

Real-World Example

Vaccination programs exemplify nonlinear influence. A small increase in vaccination rates can lead to herd immunity, preventing outbreaks and protecting even those who aren't vaccinated. This ripple effect magnifies the impact of individual actions, creating widespread health benefits.

Why It Matters

Nonlinear influences reveal where effort is best spent. Instead of spreading resources thinly across the system, you can focus on high-leverage areas that create significant outcomes. For example, addressing bottlenecks in supply chains often yields far-reaching improvements in efficiency and reliability.

Ignoring nonlinear dynamics risks overlooking critical points of influence or underestimating the consequences of small actions. For instance, neglecting early signs of climate change can lead to catastrophic consequences later.

Understanding nonlinear influences fosters smarter problem-solving. It helps you design interventions that align with the system's natural dynamics, maximizing results while minimizing effort.

Exercises

1. **Identify a Nonlinear Influence:** Think of a system you interact with, such as a workplace or community. What small actions have had an outsized impact?

2. **Plan a Cause-and-Effect Chain:** Choose a change you'd like to make and trace its potential ripple effects through the system. Where might nonlinear influences emerge?

3. **Design a High-Leverage Intervention:** Propose an action that targets a nonlinear influence in a system you're working on. How could this small change create widespread benefits?

Key Takeaway

Nonlinear influences amplify small actions. Finding these points allows you to focus efforts where they create the greatest impact.

Chapter 66: Build Strong Systems

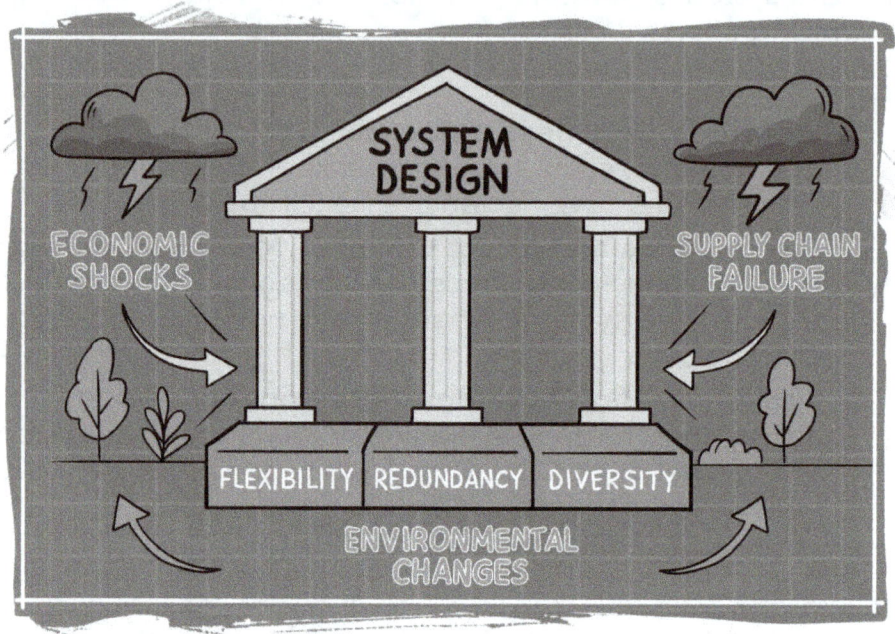

The Foundation of Resilience

Strong systems are those that endure shocks, adapt to change, and continue to function under pressure. Building such systems requires careful design, incorporating flexibility, redundancy, and diversity to withstand disruptions and recover quickly. Whether you're managing a team, designing infrastructure, or maintaining an ecosystem, building a strong system ensures long-term success.

For example, natural ecosystems like wetlands are inherently strong because they combine diverse species, self-healing mechanisms, and flexible responses to environmental changes. When a flood occurs, wetlands absorb excess water, reducing damage to nearby areas. If one species is affected, others fill its role, maintaining balance.

Strong systems aren't rigid. They're adaptable. By balancing stability with the ability to evolve, these systems navigate uncertainty while maintaining their core functions.

How to Build Strong Systems

1. **Incorporate Redundancy:** Design systems with backups for critical functions, such as alternate supply chains or multiple communication channels.

2. **Foster Flexibility:** Ensure the system can adjust to new conditions, like adaptive workflows or modular designs.

3. **Enhance Diversity:** Include a variety of components — whether species, ideas, or stakeholders — to reduce reliance on a single element.

4. **Prepare for Stress:** Identify potential disruptions and design safeguards, such as risk management plans or emergency reserves.

Real-World Example

The Internet is a strong system due to its decentralized structure. Unlike traditional communication networks with single points of failure, the internet routes data through multiple pathways. If one connection is disrupted, others ensure the system continues to function, demonstrating redundancy and adaptability.

Why It Matters

Weak systems fail under stress, while strong systems persist and evolve. For example, businesses with rigid hierarchies often struggle to adapt to market changes, while those with decentralized decision-making thrive in dynamic environments.

Building strong systems also mitigates risk. Whether in natural disasters, economic downturns, or global crises, robust systems maintain stability and provide a foundation for recovery. For instance, resilient agricultural practices — like crop diversification — reduce vulnerability to pests, weather, or market fluctuations.

Strong systems inspire confidence and collaboration. When stakeholders trust a system's durability, they're more likely to invest, innovate, and engage, creating a virtuous cycle of growth and resilience.

Exercises

1. **Assess a System's Strength:** Choose a system you rely on, such as a workplace or community. Identify its strengths and weaknesses in handling stress.

2. **Design a Stronger System:** Apply principles of redundancy, flexibility, and diversity to improve a system you're part of. How can it better withstand disruptions?

3. **Simulate a Stress Test:** Imagine a scenario that challenges a system you know. How would it respond, and what changes could make it more resilient?

Key Takeaway

Strong systems balance stability with adaptability. Building them ensures resilience in the face of uncertainty.

Chapter 67: Eliminate Obstructions

Freeing the Flow

Obstructions — whether they are physical, procedural, or systemic — disrupt the flow of energy, information, or resources in a system. These bottlenecks slow progress, create inefficiencies, and reduce overall system performance. Eliminating obstructions is critical for restoring balance, improving efficiency, and unlocking the system's full potential.

For example, in supply chains, a single overloaded warehouse can delay shipments across an entire network. By identifying and addressing this bottleneck — perhaps by redistributing inventory or improving logistics — the system regains its flow, reducing delays and improving customer satisfaction.

Obstructions can be subtle, such as outdated processes or unproductive meetings, or obvious, like a failing component in a machine. Recognizing and removing them ensures that systems operate smoothly and adapt to changing demands.

How to Eliminate Obstructions

1. **Identify Bottlenecks:** Observe where flows slow down or stop, whether it's in communication, resource distribution, or decision-making.

2. **Analyze Root Causes:** Determine what's causing the obstruction. Is it a structural issue, a process inefficiency, or a lack of resources?

3. **Engage Stakeholders:** Involve those affected by the obstruction to gather insights and ideas for resolving it.

4. **Implement and Monitor Solutions:** Apply targeted interventions to remove the bottleneck, then monitor the system to ensure the obstruction doesn't return.

Real-World Example

In software development, teams often encounter bottlenecks during code reviews, where a single reviewer is overwhelmed with tasks. To address this, companies can train additional reviewers or automate parts of the process, freeing up the flow of work and speeding up project timelines.

Why It Matters

Obstructions reduce efficiency, waste resources, and frustrate stakeholders. Eliminating them unlocks the system's potential and creates opportunities for growth and innovation. For example, streamlining approval processes in an organization can reduce delays, empowering teams to act more decisively and achieve goals faster.

Addressing obstructions also fosters resilience. Systems with fewer bottlenecks are better equipped to handle stress, adapt to change, and recover from disruptions. For instance, decentralizing decision-making in disaster response ensures that critical actions aren't delayed by a single overwhelmed authority.

Beyond practical benefits, removing obstructions improves morale and engagement. When people see their efforts flowing smoothly, they're more motivated to contribute, creating a positive cycle of productivity and collaboration.

Exercises

1. **Map a Bottleneck:** Choose a system you're part of, such as a team workflow or a household routine. Identify one bottleneck that slows progress or creates frustration.

2. **Analyze the Obstruction:** Reflect on the root causes of the bottleneck. What factors contribute to the slowdown, and how might they be addressed?

3. **Propose a Solution:** Design and implement a change to remove the bottleneck. Monitor the results and consider whether further adjustments are needed.

Key Takeaway

Eliminating obstructions restores flow and efficiency. Targeting bottlenecks unleashes the full potential of any system.

Chapter 68: Encourage Cross-System Collaboration

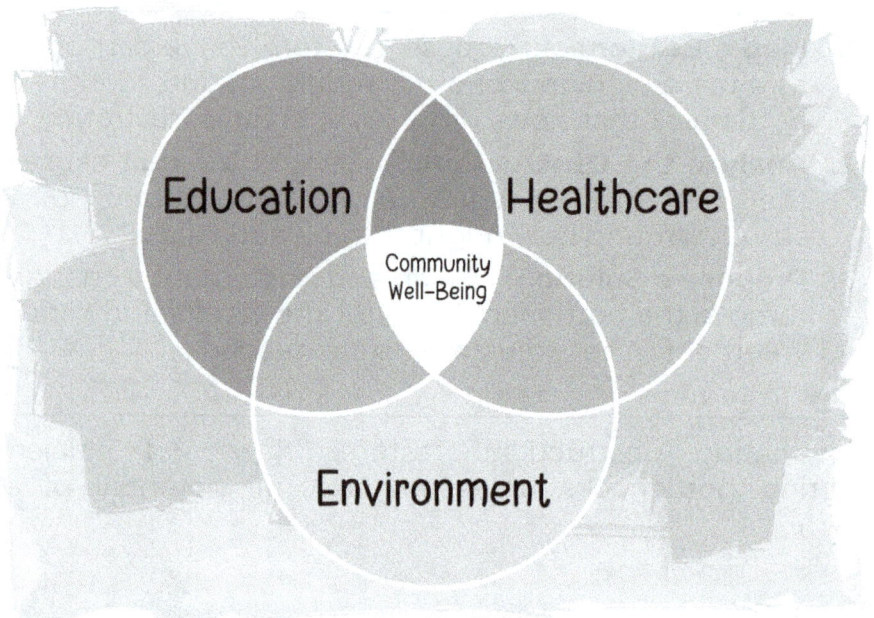

Bridging Silos for Greater Impact

No system exists in isolation. Education, healthcare, transportation, the environment — all these systems interact and influence one another. Encouraging collaboration across systems reveals shared challenges, aligns goals, and creates solutions that benefit multiple areas simultaneously. Cross-system collaboration is essential for tackling complex problems and maximizing collective impact.

For example, addressing childhood obesity requires collaboration between education (to teach nutrition), healthcare (to monitor and manage health), and urban planning (to design safe spaces for exercise). When these systems work together, their combined efforts are far more effective than isolated actions.

Collaboration often uncovers synergies and opportunities that would otherwise remain hidden. It builds a culture of partnership, breaking down silos and fostering innovation that benefits the entire ecosystem.

How to Encourage Cross-System Collaboration

1. **Identify Shared Goals:** Look for areas where systems overlap or have mutual interests, such as improving public health or reducing resource waste.
2. **Engage Stakeholders:** Bring together representatives from different systems to share perspectives, identify connections, and brainstorm solutions.
3. **Align Efforts:** Coordinate actions to ensure that interventions in one system support or amplify efforts in another.
4. **Monitor Collective Impact:** Track how collaborative efforts influence all systems involved, refining the approach as needed.

Real-World Example

During the COVID-19 pandemic, governments coordinated between public health systems, educational institutions, and technology providers to facilitate remote learning. This collaboration ensured that students could continue their education while minimizing health risks, showcasing the power of cross-system partnership.

Why It Matters

Cross-system collaboration addresses challenges more effectively than isolated efforts. For example, integrating healthcare and social services ensures that patients receive holistic care, addressing both medical needs and underlying social determinants like housing or nutrition.

Collaboration also builds resilience. Systems that communicate and support one another adapt more effectively to disruptions, ensuring continuity of services. For instance, during natural disasters, partnerships between transportation, emergency response, and local governments enable faster recovery and resource distribution.

Encouraging collaboration fosters innovation by bringing diverse perspectives and expertise to the table. It breaks down barriers, aligns resources, and creates solutions that benefit multiple stakeholders.

Exercises

1. **Identify Overlaps:** Choose two systems you interact with, such as education and healthcare. Map areas where their goals or challenges overlap.

2. **Analyze a Collaboration:** Think of an example where systems worked together successfully. What made the collaboration effective, and what lessons can be applied elsewhere?

3. **Propose a Partnership:** For a problem you want to solve, suggest a collaboration between two or more systems. Outline how they could work together and what benefits might emerge.

Key Takeaway

Cross-system collaboration amplifies impact. Breaking silos and aligning efforts creates solutions that benefit multiple systems.

Chapter 69: Monitor Leading Indicators

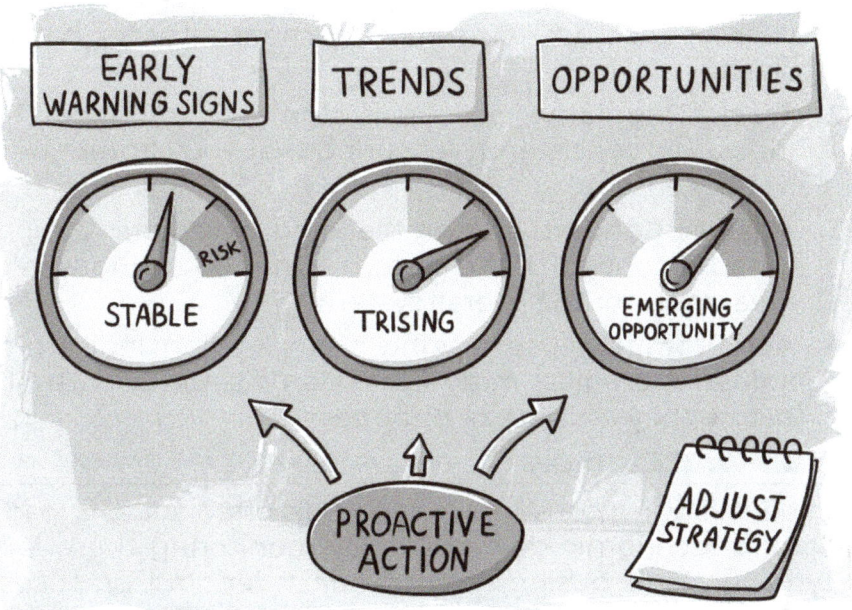

The Early Signals of Change

Leading indicators are the early warning signs that give insight into how a system is likely to behave in the future. Unlike lagging indicators, which measure past performance, leading indicators point to emerging trends, risks, or opportunities. Monitoring these signals allows you to act proactively rather than reactively, making timely adjustments that can prevent problems or capitalize on advantages.

For example, in environmental conservation, declining pollinator populations are a leading indicator of broader ecosystem stress. Acting on this early signal—by addressing habitat loss or pesticide use—can prevent cascading failures that affect food systems and biodiversity.

Leading indicators are crucial in dynamic systems where change happens quickly. By focusing on these signals, you can better predict outcomes, adapt strategies, and build resilience against potential disruptions.

How to Monitor Leading Indicators

1. **Define Key Metrics:** Identify the specific indicators that provide early insight into system performance or health, such as resource levels, engagement rates, or behavior shifts.

2. **Track Regularly:** Set up systems to monitor these indicators consistently, ensuring that you capture trends as they emerge.

3. **Analyze Context:** Interpret leading indicators within the broader context of the system. What do changes in one area imply for the overall system?

4. **Act Promptly:** Use insights from leading indicators to adjust strategies, mitigate risks, or seize opportunities before they escalate or disappear.

Real-World Example

In finance, rising consumer debt levels often act as a leading indicator of economic downturns. By monitoring these levels, policymakers and businesses can adjust lending practices or prepare for potential slowdowns, reducing the impact of future crises.

Why It Matters

Monitoring leading indicators helps you stay ahead of change. Waiting for lagging indicators to confirm problems often means it's too late to prevent or minimize damage. For example, monitoring hospital admission trends during a disease outbreak allows health systems to prepare resources before cases peak, saving lives.

Leading indicators also uncover opportunities for innovation or growth. For instance, tracking user engagement on a new platform can reveal trends that guide future development, ensuring the system evolves in line with user needs.

This proactive approach reduces uncertainty and builds confidence in decision-making. It enables systems to adapt dynamically, responding to emerging signals instead of being blindsided by unexpected changes.

Exercises

1. **Identify a Leading Indicator:** Think of a system you're part of, such as a workplace or community project. What early signals could predict future success or challenges?

2. **Track a Trend:** Choose a metric to monitor over time, such as customer feedback or resource usage. Reflect on what changes in this indicator reveal about the system.

3. **Design a Monitoring Plan:** For a goal or system you're managing, outline a strategy to track and act on leading indicators. How will this plan keep you ahead of change?

Key Takeaway

Leading indicators are your early-warning system. Monitoring them enables proactive adjustments and better decision-making.

Chapter 70: Avoid Over-Optimization

The Danger of Perfect Efficiency

Optimizing systems for maximum efficiency often seems like the ultimate goal. However, over-optimization can make systems brittle and vulnerable to disruptions. When every resource is used to its fullest capacity, there's no room for error, adaptation, or recovery, creating a system that's efficient but fragile.

Consider a factory operating with just-in-time inventory systems. While this reduces storage costs and improves efficiency, it leaves no buffer for supply chain delays. When a disruption occurs, such as a shipping delay or resource shortage, production grinds to a halt, revealing the hidden cost of over-optimization.

Striking a balance between efficiency and resilience is critical for building systems that are both high-performing and adaptable. Flexibility, redundancy, and safety margins may seem inefficient in the short term, but they are essential for long-term stability.

How to Avoid Over-Optimization

1. **Build Buffers:** Include safety margins in your system, such as backup resources, extra time, or redundant processes.

2. **Prioritize Resilience:** Balance efficiency with the ability to absorb shocks, adapt to change, and recover from setbacks.

3. **Test System Limits:** Regularly evaluate how the system performs under stress. Are there points where it becomes fragile?

4. **Plan for Uncertainty:** Design systems that can handle variability, whether it's fluctuating demand, environmental changes, or unexpected disruptions.

Real-World Example

In agriculture, monoculture farming is often optimized for maximum yield, focusing on a single crop. However, this approach makes farms highly vulnerable to pests, diseases, and climate fluctuations. By incorporating crop rotation and biodiversity — practices seen as less "efficient" — farmers build resilience, ensuring long-term productivity.

Why It Matters

Over-optimization sacrifices adaptability for short-term gains. While streamlined processes may work well in stable conditions, they fail under stress, leading to costly disruptions or even system collapse. For instance, power grids optimized without redundancy are more likely to experience widespread blackouts during high demand or equipment failures.

Balancing efficiency with resilience creates systems that perform well without compromising their ability to adapt. For example, businesses that maintain reserve funds or diversified supply chains are better equipped to weather economic downturns or market changes.

Recognizing the hidden costs of over-optimization helps you design systems that prioritize long-term sustainability over short-term perfection.

Exercises

1. **Assess a System's Flexibility:** Choose a system you know and evaluate whether it has room for adaptation or recovery. What changes could make it less fragile?

2. **Analyze Over-Optimization:** Reflect on a time when efficiency was prioritized over resilience. What were the consequences, and how could they have been mitigated?

3. **Design for Balance:** For a project or system, propose ways to balance efficiency with flexibility, ensuring it can handle uncertainty.

Key Takeaway

Over-optimization sacrifices resilience for short-term gains. Balancing efficiency with flexibility ensures long-term system stability.

Chapter 71: Develop Iterative Solutions

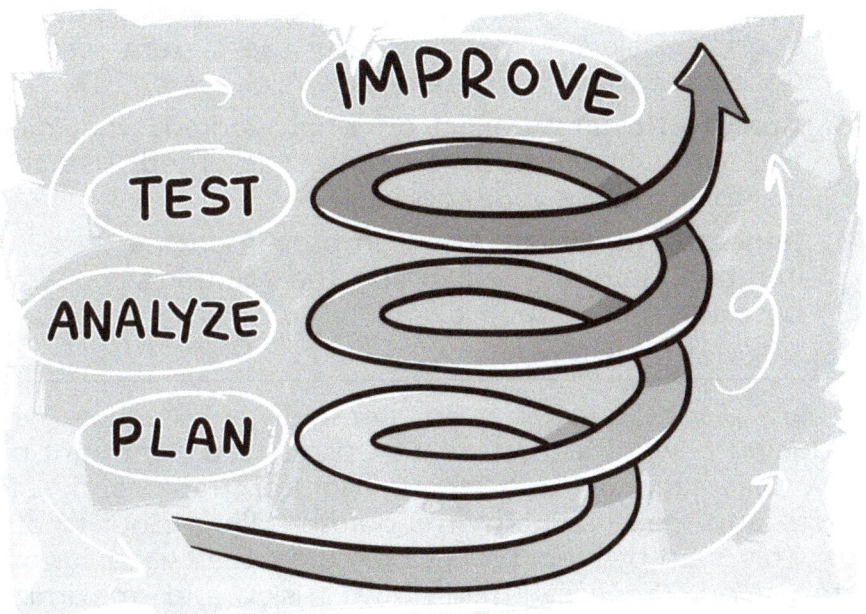

Progress Through Iteration

In complex systems, solutions are rarely perfect on the first try. Iterative solutions embrace the idea of continuous refinement: starting with an initial idea, testing it, learning from results, and improving the approach in cycles. This method is particularly useful in dynamic or unpredictable systems, where conditions evolve and new challenges emerge.

Consider the development of mobile apps. Developers release a basic version (the minimum viable product), gather user feedback, and release updates to address bugs, add features, and enhance usability. Over time, the app evolves into a polished product that aligns with user needs, all thanks to iterative improvement.

Iteration fosters adaptability. Instead of waiting for a perfect plan, it allows you to act, learn, and adjust in real-time, ensuring that solutions remain relevant and effective.

How to Develop Iterative Solutions

1. **Start Small:** Begin with a basic version of your solution that addresses core needs without overcomplicating the design.

2. **Test and Gather Feedback:** Implement your solution on a small scale and monitor how the system responds. Collect feedback from stakeholders or users.

3. **Analyze Results:** Reflect on what worked, what didn't, and what unexpected outcomes emerged. Use these insights to refine your approach.

4. **Repeat and Scale:** Apply improvements in the next iteration, gradually expanding the solution's scope as it becomes more effective.

Real-World Example

Urban planners often use iterative approaches when introducing new infrastructure. For instance, a city might pilot a new bike lane on one street, monitor traffic and safety impacts, and make adjustments before rolling it out to other areas. This step-by-step process ensures that each iteration improves on the last, minimizing risks and maximizing benefits.

Why It Matters

Iterative solutions prioritize learning and adaptability, making them ideal for complex systems where static plans often fail. For example, in education, iterative approaches allow teachers to refine lesson plans based on student performance and feedback, improving outcomes over time.

Iteration also reduces the pressure to "get it right" the first time. By breaking solutions into manageable cycles, you can make progress without being paralyzed by the fear of failure. Each iteration builds on the last, creating a sense of momentum and continuous improvement.

This approach is also highly inclusive. Involving stakeholders in each phase of iteration ensures that solutions address diverse perspectives and needs, resulting in more equitable and effective outcomes.

Exercises

1. **Apply Iteration to a Goal:** Choose a project or problem you're working on and outline an iterative plan. What small step can you test first, and how will you refine it?

2. **Analyze Past Iteration:** Reflect on a time when you refined a process or solution over multiple attempts. What did you learn, and how did the iterations improve the outcome?

3. **Design a Feedback Loop for Iteration:** Identify how you'll gather feedback and measure success at each stage of an iterative project.

Key Takeaway

Iterative solutions embrace cycles of learning and improvement—this approach ensures adaptability and progress in dynamic systems.

Chapter 72: Align Incentives

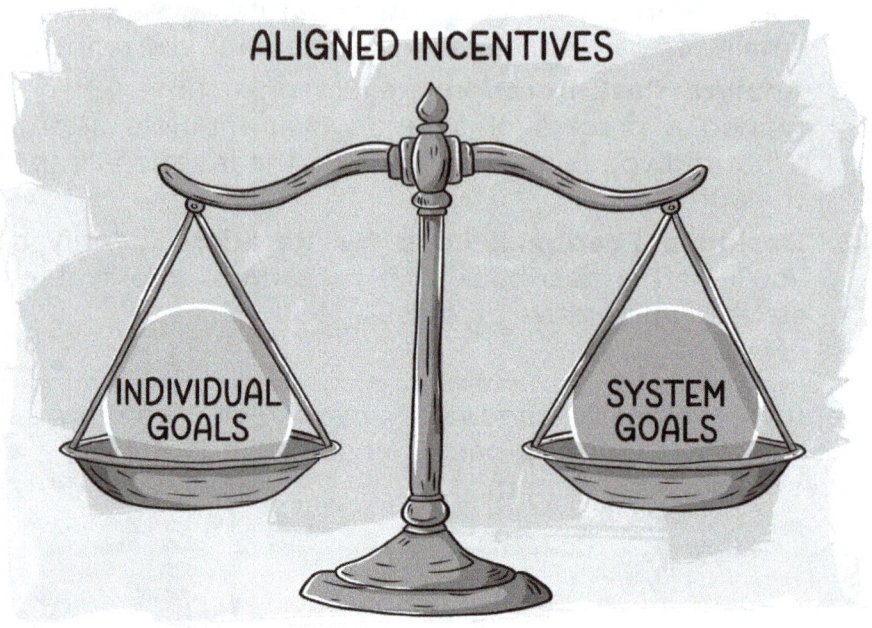

ALIGNED INCENTIVES

INDIVIDUAL GOALS

SYSTEM GOALS

Motivating for Mutual Success

Incentives are the forces that drive behavior in a system, whether financial rewards, recognition, or intrinsic motivations. Aligning incentives means ensuring that individual goals are in harmony with the broader system's objectives. When incentives are misaligned, actions that benefit individuals may harm the system, leading to inefficiencies, conflict, or even collapse.

For example, in a workplace, if employees are rewarded solely for individual sales, they may prioritize personal gains over teamwork, harming customer satisfaction or long-term business growth. Aligning incentives — such as rewarding both individual performance and team collaboration — encourages behaviors that benefit both the individual and the organization.

This principle applies across systems, from public policy to ecosystems. By aligning motivations with desired outcomes, you create a system that naturally drives toward its goals.

How to Align Incentives

1. **Understand Current Motivations:** Identify what drives behavior in the system. Are these incentives leading to desired outcomes or unintended consequences?
2. **Define System Goals:** Clearly articulate what the system is trying to achieve, such as efficiency, sustainability, or equity.
3. **Create Shared Benefits:** Design incentives that reward actions benefiting both individuals and the system as a whole.
4. **Monitor and Adjust:** Continuously evaluate whether incentives are achieving their intended effects, and make adjustments as needed.

Real-World Example

In environmental conservation, carbon credit systems align financial incentives with sustainability goals. Companies that reduce emissions can sell credits to others, creating a financial motive for sustainable practices. This approach balances individual profit with global environmental benefits.

Why It Matters

Misaligned incentives create friction and inefficiencies, often driving behaviors that undermine the system's goals. For example, healthcare providers paid solely for the volume of procedures may prioritize quantity over quality, leading to over-treatment and higher costs. Aligning incentives with patient outcomes ensures better care and system efficiency.

Aligned incentives also build trust and collaboration. When stakeholders see that their interests are considered, they're more likely to engage constructively and work toward shared goals. This principle is particularly important in systems with diverse actors, such as communities or multinational organizations.

By designing incentives thoughtfully, you create a system that naturally moves toward success, reducing the need for constant oversight or correction.

Exercises

1. **Analyze a System's Incentives:** Choose a system you're part of, such as a workplace or community group. Are incentives aligned with the system's goals, or do they create conflict?

2. **Redesign Incentives:** For a system with misaligned incentives, propose changes that balance individual motivations with system-wide benefits.

3. **Track Incentive Impacts:** Implement a new incentive in a system you manage and observe how it changes behavior over time.

Key Takeaway

Aligning incentives ensures that individual actions support system-wide goals, creating harmony and driving collective success.

Chapter 73: Broaden Your Scope of Analysis

SHIFT PERSPECTIVE

Seeing the Bigger Picture

When solving problems or understanding systems, it's easy to focus too narrowly, analyzing only the most obvious elements or immediate factors. While this can yield quick insights, it often misses the larger context where true solutions lie. Broadening your scope of analysis involves stepping back to consider external influences, indirect connections, and long-term impacts. This approach ensures that you capture the full complexity of the system and avoid unintended consequences.

For example, when addressing urban traffic congestion, analyzing only road layouts may overlook broader factors like public transportation availability, population growth, and urban planning policies. Expanding the scope to include these elements can lead to more comprehensive and sustainable solutions, such as investing in mass transit or designing walkable neighborhoods.

Broadening your scope doesn't mean overcomplicating your analysis. Instead, it's about looking at the system in context, ensuring that every piece of the puzzle is considered before making decisions.

How to Broaden Your Scope

1. **Identify External Influences:** Ask what factors outside the immediate system might be affecting its behavior, such as economic trends, environmental changes, or cultural shifts.

2. **Map Interconnections:** Analyze how the system interacts with neighboring systems, such as how a supply chain depends on global trade or how an ecosystem interacts with urban development.

3. **Consider Long-Term Effects:** Look beyond short-term outcomes to evaluate how decisions might impact the system over time.

4. **Engage Diverse Perspectives:** Consult stakeholders from different fields or backgrounds to uncover blind spots and gain a more holistic view.

Real-World Example

In public health, addressing obesity requires a broad analysis that includes not only individual behaviors but also factors like food deserts, cultural norms, economic inequality, and urban design. Solutions that target these broader influences — such as creating policies for healthier food access — are far more effective than those focused solely on individual choices.

Why It Matters

Narrow analyses often lead to incomplete solutions or unintended consequences. For instance, focusing solely on expanding roads to reduce traffic might encourage more car usage, worsening congestion in the long run. Broadening your scope reveals alternative solutions, such as improving public transit or incentivizing carpooling.

This approach also enhances adaptability. Systems rarely operate in isolation, and external changes can disrupt even well-designed plans. By considering the bigger picture, you prepare for these shifts and ensure that solutions remain effective under changing conditions.

Finally, a broader scope fosters collaboration. When all interconnected elements are on the table, diverse stakeholders can align their efforts, creating solutions that benefit the entire ecosystem.

Exercises

1. **Expand an Analysis:** Choose a system you're analyzing, such as a workplace process or community issue. Identify factors outside the immediate system that could influence its behavior.

2. **Make Connections:** Create a diagram showing how your system interacts with neighboring systems or external forces. Reflect on what these connections reveal.

3. **Think Long-Term:** For a decision you're considering, imagine how it might affect the system five, ten, or twenty years from now. Does your solution hold up over time?

Key Takeaway

Broadening your scope of analysis reveals hidden connections and external influences. This holistic approach ensures more effective and sustainable solutions.

Chapter 74: Reduce Delays in Reporting

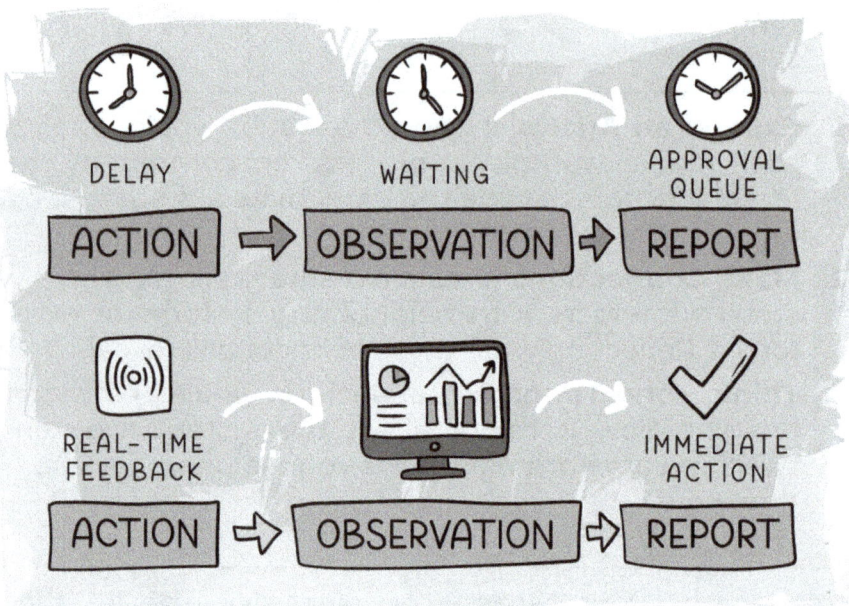

Timely Information, Better Decisions

In systems where decisions rely on feedback, delays in reporting create blind spots that lead to inefficiencies, poor outcomes, or even crises. Reducing these delays ensures that decision-makers receive accurate and timely information, allowing them to respond effectively and keep the system on track.

For instance, in disaster response, slow reporting of damages or resource needs can delay aid distribution, worsening the situation. Streamlining reporting processes — through real-time data collection or automated systems — improves coordination and ensures that help arrives when and where it's needed.

Timely reporting isn't just about speed; it's also about relevance. Information must be accurate, actionable, and delivered to the right people at the right time to make a difference.

How to Reduce Delays in Reporting

1. **Streamline Communication Channels:** Minimize unnecessary steps between data collection and decision-making, such as redundant approvals or manual reporting processes.

2. **Leverage Technology:** Use tools like sensors, dashboards, or real-time analytics to automate data collection and reporting.

3. **Prioritize Key Metrics:** Focus on collecting and sharing the most critical information, avoiding overload or distractions from less relevant data.

4. **Establish Clear Roles:** Assign responsibilities for data collection, validation, and reporting to ensure accountability and reduce bottlenecks.

Real-World Example

In manufacturing, real-time monitoring systems alert operators to equipment malfunctions as they occur. This immediate reporting allows for quick intervention, preventing costly downtime or further damage. In contrast, delayed reporting might result in extended shutdowns or safety risks.

Why It Matters

Delayed reporting often leads to missed opportunities or preventable failures. For example, in financial systems, outdated reports might cause investors to act on irrelevant data, leading to poor decisions or missed market opportunities. Faster reporting ensures that actions are based on current realities, not past conditions.

Reducing delays also improves system resilience. When disruptions occur, timely feedback allows for rapid adjustments, minimizing damage and restoring balance. For instance, during a supply chain disruption, real-time updates on inventory levels enable faster rerouting of resources, reducing losses.

Beyond practical benefits, streamlined reporting fosters trust and accountability. When stakeholders have access to accurate and timely information, transparency increases, and decision-making becomes more collaborative and effective.

Exercises

1. **Analyze Reporting Delays:** Choose a system you're part of, such as a workplace or community project. Identify points where delays in reporting slow down decision-making.

2. **Propose Improvements:** Design changes to reduce reporting delays, such as automating data collection or simplifying communication channels.

3. **Track Results:** Implement your changes and monitor how they impact decision-making speed and quality. Reflect on lessons learned.

Key Takeaway

Reducing delays in reporting ensures timely, accurate information. This accelerates decision-making and enhances system performance.

Chapter 75: Encourage Transparency

Clarity Creates Trust

Transparency is essential for effective systems management. It means making processes, decisions, and flows within a system clear and accessible to everyone involved. When stakeholders understand how the system works — how resources move, how decisions are made, and what outcomes are expected — they can make better contributions and hold the system accountable.

For instance, in public budgeting, transparent systems that show where funds come from and how they are spent foster trust among citizens. This clarity helps avoid misunderstandings, reduces corruption, and allows for more informed participation in decision-making.

Transparency also ensures that potential inefficiencies, risks, or conflicts are spotted early. Without it, problems often remain hidden until they escalate, making them harder and costlier to address.

How to Encourage Transparency

1. **Document Processes Clearly:** Map out how the system functions, using diagrams or flowcharts to make information accessible to all stakeholders.

2. **Share Data Openly:** Make critical information, such as metrics, decisions, or outcomes, easily available to those who need it. Use dashboards, reports, or meetings to share updates.

3. **Eliminate Black Boxes:** Avoid processes or areas within the system that are opaque or understood by only a few individuals. Encourage knowledge sharing and collaboration.

4. **Solicit Feedback:** Actively seek input from stakeholders to ensure that transparency efforts are meeting their needs and that no information is being overlooked.

Real-World Example

In supply chain management, transparency is a growing focus. Companies use blockchain technology to track the movement of goods, providing real-time visibility into where products come from, how they're handled, and when they'll arrive. This level of transparency builds trust between suppliers, businesses, and customers.

Why It Matters

Without transparency, systems are prone to inefficiency, corruption, and conflict. For example, organizations with opaque decision-making processes often experience confusion or resentment among employees, reducing morale and productivity. Transparency ensures that everyone understands the goals and operations of the system, fostering alignment and collaboration.

Transparency also enhances accountability. When stakeholders can see how their actions impact the system and how the system serves its goals, they're more likely to act responsibly. This principle applies to everything from corporate governance to community initiatives.

Moreover, transparency strengthens trust. Whether between government and citizens, businesses and customers, or leaders and teams, clear communication and open access to information build confidence and mutual respect.

Exercises

1. **Evaluate Transparency:** Choose a system you interact with, such as a workplace or local government. Identify areas where transparency is strong and where it could be improved.

2. **Create a Transparency Plan:** For a project or system you manage, outline steps to make processes, data, or decisions clearer to stakeholders.

3. **Monitor Transparency's Impact:** Implement changes to improve transparency and track how they affect trust, efficiency, or collaboration within the system.

Key Takeaway

Transparency fosters trust, accountability, and efficiency. Making systems clear and accessible empowers stakeholders and improves outcomes.

Chapter 76: Counteract Perverse Incentives

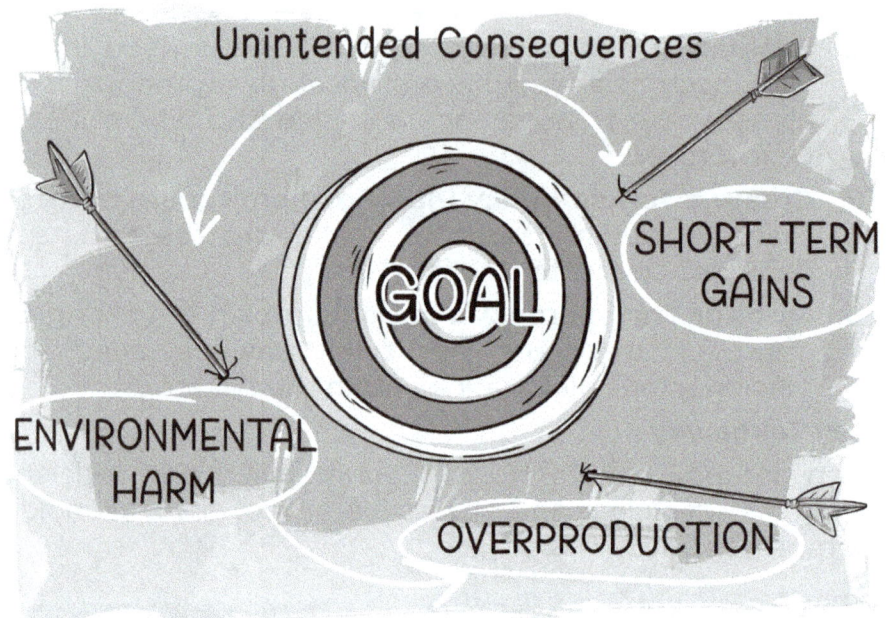

When Incentives Go Awry

Perverse incentives are rewards or penalties that unintentionally encourage behaviors harmful to the system's overall goals. These misaligned motivations often arise from poorly designed policies, metrics, or structures, and they can have far-reaching consequences if left unchecked.

For example, a factory rewarded for producing the highest volume of goods might prioritize quantity over quality, leading to defective products and dissatisfied customers. Similarly, teachers judged solely on student test scores may focus on rote memorization rather than fostering critical thinking.

Counteracting perverse incentives requires carefully aligning rewards and penalties with desired outcomes. This ensures that individual actions support, rather than undermine, the system's broader objectives.

How to Counteract Perverse Incentives

1. **Identify Misaligned Rewards:** Analyze the system to find incentives that lead to unintended consequences, such as focusing on short-term gains at the expense of long-term goals.

2. **Clarify Desired Outcomes:** Define the system's objectives clearly, ensuring that incentives align with achieving these goals.

3. **Redesign Incentive Structures:** Adjust rewards and penalties to encourage behaviors that benefit the system as a whole.

4. **Monitor and Refine:** Continuously evaluate how incentives impact the system, making adjustments as needed to maintain alignment.

Real-World Example

In fisheries management, quotas designed to prevent overfishing sometimes create a "race to fish," where fleets rush to catch their limits before others, leading to unsafe practices and resource depletion. Transitioning to catch-share programs, where fishermen hold rights to a percentage of the total allowable catch, aligns incentives with sustainability, encouraging careful resource management.

Why It Matters

Perverse incentives undermine trust, efficiency, and long-term success. For instance, in healthcare, fee-for-service payment models can incentivize unnecessary treatments, driving up costs without improving patient outcomes. Addressing these misalignments ensures that the system serves its intended purpose effectively.

Aligned incentives also prevent resource waste. When motivations align with goals, resources are used more efficiently, and efforts are focused where they're most needed. For example, companies that reward innovation rather than excessive cost-cutting are more likely to thrive in competitive markets.

Counteracting perverse incentives fosters a culture of accountability and alignment. Stakeholders are more engaged and motivated when they see that their efforts contribute to meaningful and constructive outcomes.

Exercises

1. **Identify a Perverse Incentive:** Reflect on a system you're familiar with, such as a workplace policy or community initiative. Are there incentives that unintentionally encourage harmful behaviors?

2. **Redesign Incentives:** Propose changes to align rewards and penalties with the system's goals. How would these adjustments improve outcomes?

3. **Track Impact:** Implement a redesigned incentive and monitor its effects on behavior and system performance. What lessons can you apply moving forward?

Key Takeaway

Misaligned incentives lead to unintended consequences. Realigning them ensures that actions support the system's overall goals.

Chapter 77: Use Systems Thinking in Leadership

Leading Through Connection

Leadership in complex systems requires more than managing tasks or achieving immediate goals. It demands a holistic perspective—understanding how decisions ripple across interconnected parts and considering long-term impacts. Systems thinking equips leaders to anticipate challenges, identify opportunities, and align diverse components toward shared objectives.

Consider a CEO leading a company through digital transformation. A systems-thinking leader wouldn't just focus on implementing new technologies. They'd analyze how these changes impact employee workflows, customer experiences, and the broader market. By addressing these interconnected elements, they'd create a smoother transition that benefits the entire organization.

Effective leaders use systems thinking to foster collaboration, adapt to change, and ensure sustainable success. Instead of treating problems in isolation, they see the bigger picture, guiding their teams with clarity and purpose.

How to Use Systems Thinking in Leadership

1. **Develop a Holistic Vision:** Focus on the big picture, considering how decisions impact all parts of the system and their stakeholders.

2. **Engage Stakeholders:** Involve team members, partners, and communities in decision-making to gather diverse perspectives and build alignment.

3. **Anticipate Ripple Effects:** Analyze how short-term actions might create long-term consequences, ensuring that strategies align with the system's goals.

4. **Promote Adaptability:** Design systems and teams that can adjust to changing circumstances, ensuring resilience in the face of uncertainty.

Real-World Example

Jacinda Ardern, former Prime Minister of New Zealand, applied systems thinking during the COVID-19 pandemic. Her leadership balanced public health measures, economic stability, and social well-being, creating a coordinated response that minimized harm across interconnected systems. By engaging communities and considering diverse needs, she guided her country with empathy and effectiveness.

Why It Matters

Systems-thinking leaders create stability in complexity. When decisions are made without understanding how they affect interconnected parts, unintended consequences arise. For example, a company that cuts costs by downsizing staff might see short-term financial gains but suffer long-term productivity losses due to employee burnout and decreased morale.

Leadership grounded in systems thinking ensures that strategies are sustainable. By addressing root causes rather than symptoms, leaders create solutions that endure over time. For instance, a mayor improving urban transportation might focus not just on building roads but also on integrating public transit, walkable spaces, and bike lanes for a comprehensive solution.

Systems thinking also fosters collaboration. Leaders who see the connections between diverse stakeholders can build partnerships that amplify impact, aligning efforts toward common goals.

Exercises

1. **Analyze a Leadership Challenge:** Reflect on a complex decision you've faced or observed. How might systems thinking have changed the approach or outcome?

2. **Create a Systems Structure:** For a team or project you lead, map out the interconnections between people, processes, and goals. Use these guidelines to identify potential ripple effects.

3. **Practice Holistic Decision-Making:** Choose an upcoming decision and consider its short-term and long-term impacts on the system. How can you align it with broader goals?

Key Takeaway

Systems-thinking leaders see the big picture, anticipate ripple effects, and guide their teams with clarity and purpose, ensuring sustainable success.

Chapter 78: Apply Risk Management Systems

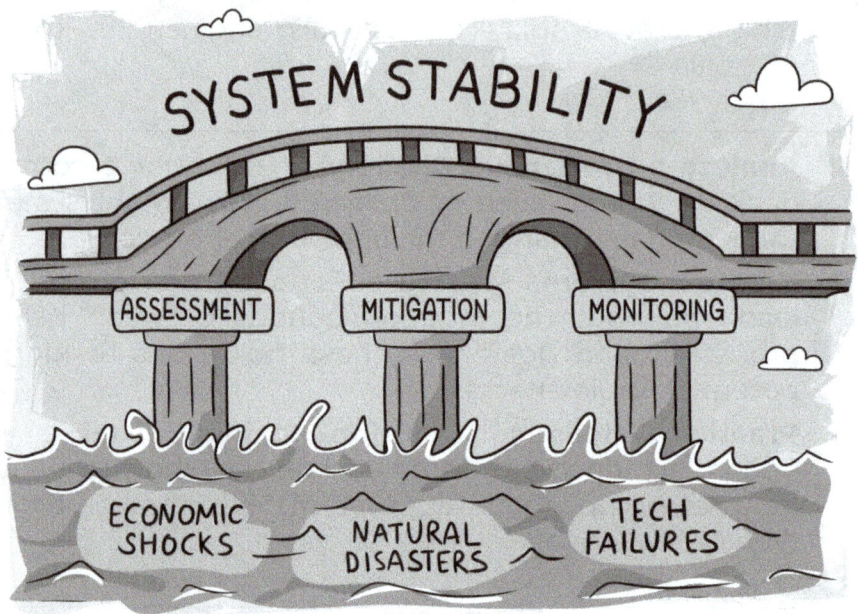

Planning for the Unexpected

Every system faces risks — uncertainties that can disrupt its stability and performance. Risk management systems identify these potential threats, assess their likelihood and impact, and implement strategies to minimize harm. This proactive approach ensures that systems remain resilient, even in the face of disruptions.

Consider an energy company preparing for natural disasters. By identifying risks like hurricanes or droughts, assessing their potential to disrupt power grids, and implementing strategies like backup generators or grid diversification, the company can maintain services during crises.

Risk management isn't just about avoiding harm. It's about building systems that can adapt and recover. This approach fosters confidence and stability, ensuring that systems thrive even under challenging conditions.

How to Apply Risk Management Systems

1. **Identify Potential Risks:** Map out vulnerabilities in the system, such as resource dependencies, external pressures, or technological weaknesses.

2. **Assess Likelihood and Impact:** Evaluate how likely each risk is to occur and how severely it would affect the system. Prioritize high-impact risks.

3. **Develop Mitigation Strategies:** Create plans to reduce the likelihood or minimize the impact of key risks, such as diversifying suppliers or implementing redundancies.

4. **Monitor and Adapt:** Continuously track risks and update strategies as conditions change or new vulnerabilities emerge.

Real-World Example

In financial systems, stress tests simulate adverse scenarios — such as market crashes or interest rate spikes — to assess banks' resilience. These tests help institutions identify vulnerabilities and implement safeguards, such as maintaining higher capital reserves, ensuring stability during economic turbulence.

Why It Matters

Risk management systems protect against disruptions that can derail progress or cause significant harm. For example, a hospital without adequate risk management might run out of critical supplies during a pandemic, compromising patient care. Proactive planning ensures that resources are available when needed.

Effective risk management also enhances decision-making. By understanding potential threats, leaders can make informed choices that balance opportunities with safeguards. For instance, a company entering a new market might mitigate risks by piloting its product in a small region before expanding.

Beyond immediate benefits, risk management builds trust. Stakeholders are more likely to invest, collaborate, or participate when they see that systems are prepared for uncertainties.

Exercises

1. **Identify Risks in a System:** Choose a system you're part of and list potential risks it faces. Which are the most likely or impactful?

2. **Propose Mitigation Strategies:** For one key risk, design a plan to reduce its likelihood or impact. Consider redundancies, diversification, or contingency plans.

3. **Monitor Risks Over Time:** Implement a risk management plan and track its effectiveness. Adjust your strategies as conditions evolve.

Key Takeaway

Risk management systems protect against disruptions, ensuring that systems remain resilient and prepared for uncertainties.

Chapter 79: Strengthen Weak Connections

The Power of Connectivity

In any system, connections between components determine how well it functions. While strong connections foster collaboration, resilience, and efficiency, weak connections can create bottlenecks, reduce performance, and leave the system vulnerable to stress. Strengthening these weak links ensures that the entire system works cohesively and can handle disruptions more effectively.

For example, in a workplace, weak connections might appear as departments that rarely communicate, leading to misunderstandings or missed opportunities. Strengthening these links—perhaps through cross-department meetings or shared goals — improves collaboration, prevents inefficiencies, and drives innovation.

Weak connections often go unnoticed until a crisis exposes their fragility. By identifying and reinforcing them proactively, you create a system that's not only efficient but also adaptable and robust.

How to Strengthen Weak Connections

1. **Identify Fragile Links:** Map out the connections in your system and look for areas where communication, trust, or resources are lacking.

2. **Foster Collaboration:** Build bridges between disconnected parts of the system, such as through joint projects, regular meetings, or shared platforms.

3. **Invest in Resources:** Provide the tools, training, or support needed to strengthen weak connections, ensuring that all components can function effectively.

4. **Monitor and Adapt:** Continuously assess the strength of connections and adjust strategies as the system evolves or new weak points emerge.

Real-World Example

In supply chains, weak connections often appear as small, specialized suppliers that lack the capacity to meet surging demand. Strengthening these links — through financial support, training, or diversification of suppliers — reduces vulnerabilities and ensures smoother operations during disruptions.

Why It Matters

Weak connections are often the first points to fail during stress, causing cascading disruptions. For instance, in ecosystems, a decline in pollinator populations weakens connections between plants and insects, threatening food production and biodiversity. Addressing these weak links stabilizes the entire system.

Strengthening weak connections also promotes equity and inclusivity. In social systems, marginalized groups often represent weak connections due to limited access to resources or opportunities. By investing in these connections, systems become more equitable and resilient.

Finally, strong connections amplify the system's overall capacity. When all components are well-linked, they can share resources, coordinate efforts, and adapt more effectively to change.

Exercises

1. **Visualize Your System:** Create a diagram of the connections in a system you're part of, such as a workplace or community. Identify areas where connections are weak.

2. **Design a Strengthening Plan:** Choose one weak connection and outline steps to improve it, such as through communication, collaboration, or resource investment.

3. **Evaluate Progress:** Implement your plan and monitor how strengthening the connection impacts the system's overall performance.

Key Takeaway

Weak connections undermine systems. Identifying and strengthening them ensures resilience, equity, and cohesion.

Chapter 80: Design for Redundancy

Why Redundancy Matters

Redundancy often gets a bad reputation as inefficiency, but in systems thinking, it's a critical feature of resilience. Redundancy ensures that if one part of the system fails, others can take over, preventing total collapse. Whether it's backup servers in IT, alternative energy sources in power grids, or cross-trained employees in a workplace, redundancy allows systems to absorb shocks and recover quickly.

For example, during the COVID-19 pandemic, healthcare systems with redundant resources — like reserve staff and extra hospital beds — were better equipped to handle surges in patient numbers. Without these backups, many systems faced critical failures.

Designing for redundancy involves identifying critical functions, assessing vulnerabilities, and creating overlaps or backups that keep the system running smoothly, even under stress.

How to Design for Redundancy

1. **Identify Critical Functions:** Determine which parts of the system are essential for its operation, such as key processes, resources, or roles.

2. **Assess Vulnerabilities:** Analyze where failures are most likely to occur, whether from external disruptions or internal weaknesses.

3. **Build Backup Systems:** Create alternatives, such as duplicate resources, cross-training employees, or parallel processes, to ensure continuity.

4. **Test Redundancies:** Regularly evaluate how well backup systems perform under simulated stress, making improvements as needed.

Real-World Example

Airlines build redundancy into their safety systems by having duplicate instruments, backup pilots, and multiple layers of checks. If one system fails, another takes over, ensuring passenger safety and preventing catastrophic failures.

Why It Matters

Without redundancy, systems are brittle and prone to collapse when disruptions occur. For example, a factory with no backup machinery might lose weeks of production if a critical component breaks down. Redundancy provides the flexibility and resilience needed to adapt and recover.

Redundancy also creates opportunities for innovation. In workplaces, cross-training employees not only builds backup capacity but also enhances team versatility and collaboration. Similarly, diversified energy sources, like solar and wind, reduce reliance on fossil fuels while advancing sustainability.

Finally, redundancy fosters trust. Stakeholders feel more confident in systems designed to withstand stress, whether they're investors in a company, members of a community, or users of a service.

Exercises

1. **Identify Key Vulnerabilities:** In a system you manage, determine where failures are most likely to occur and what the consequences would be.

2. **Propose a Redundancy Plan:** Design backups or alternatives for one critical function, such as duplicate resources or cross-trained staff.

3. **Test and Evaluate:** Simulate a failure scenario to see how well your redundancy plan performs. Refine the plan as needed.

Key Takeaway

Redundancy isn't waste — it's resilience. Designing systems with backups ensures continuity and stability under stress.

Chapter 81: Avoid Unintended Consequences

Beyond the Immediate Outcome

When making decisions in complex systems, it's easy to focus on immediate goals without considering broader ripple effects. However, these systems are interconnected, and actions often produce unintended consequences — outcomes that weren't planned or desired. Understanding and anticipating these effects is critical for designing solutions that work holistically.

For example, introducing invasive species to control pests has often backfired in ecosystems. Cane toads were introduced to Australia to manage sugarcane pests, but they became a destructive force, outcompeting native species and disrupting local ecosystems. The lack of foresight about the ripple effects turned a solution into a larger problem.

Avoiding unintended consequences doesn't mean predicting every possible outcome — it means adopting a mindset of caution, curiosity, and adaptability to minimize harm and adjust strategies as needed.

How to Avoid Unintended Consequences

1. **Map the System:** Identify how different parts of the system are connected and how changes in one area might affect others.

2. **Engage Diverse Stakeholders:** Consult people with different perspectives and expertise to uncover potential ripple effects you might overlook.

3. **Simulate Scenarios:** Use tools like modeling or role-playing to explore how a decision could play out under different conditions.

4. **Monitor and Adapt:** Once an action is implemented, track its effects closely, looking for signs of unintended consequences and adjusting as needed.

Real-World Example

In urban planning, building highways to reduce traffic congestion often leads to increased car usage — a phenomenon known as induced demand. This unintended consequence worsens the very problem it aims to solve. Cities that prioritize public transit and walkability avoid this trap, creating sustainable solutions that align with broader goals.

Why It Matters

Ignoring unintended consequences can create inefficiencies, inequities, or even crises. For example, agricultural subsidies meant to stabilize food production often encourage overproduction, leading to wasted resources and environmental harm. Anticipating these effects ensures that policies and actions serve their intended purpose without creating new challenges.

Understanding unintended consequences also fosters long-term thinking. Short-term fixes may seem appealing, but they often come at the expense of sustainability. By analyzing ripple effects, you can design solutions that balance immediate needs with future impacts.

Finally, this approach builds trust and credibility. When stakeholders see that decisions are thoughtful and account for potential risks, they're more likely to support and participate in the system.

Exercises

1. **Analyze Past Decisions:** Reflect on a policy or action that produced unintended consequences. What were the ripple effects, and how could they have been anticipated?

2. **Simulate a Decision:** Choose a potential action and consider its possible outcomes, both intended and unintended. How could you minimize negative effects?

3. **Develop an Adaptive Plan:** For a current challenge, design a strategy that includes monitoring and adjustment phases to address unintended consequences as they arise.

Key Takeaway

Actions in complex systems often have ripple effects. Anticipating and addressing unintended consequences ensures thoughtful, effective solutions.

Chapter 82: Enhance System Flexibility

The Need for Adaptability

Flexibility is the hallmark of resilient systems. In a world of constant change — economic shifts, technological advances, climate fluctuations — rigid systems often fail because they can't adjust to new conditions. Flexible systems, on the other hand, absorb shocks, adapt to challenges, and thrive in dynamic environments.

For instance, during the COVID-19 pandemic, companies with flexible work policies quickly transitioned to remote operations, maintaining productivity and supporting employee well-being. Organizations with rigid structures struggled to adapt, facing disruptions in workflows and employee satisfaction.

Flexibility doesn't mean abandoning structure or planning. It means designing systems with built-in capacity to adjust, ensuring they remain effective even under uncertainty.

How to Enhance System Flexibility

1. **Diversify Resources:** Avoid over-reliance on a single resource, supplier, or process. Diversity provides alternatives when disruptions occur.

2. **Embrace Modular Design:** Break systems into smaller, independent components that can be adjusted or replaced without disrupting the entire system.

3. **Encourage Experimentation:** Foster a culture of innovation where testing new ideas and learning from failures is embraced.

4. **Build Feedback Mechanisms:** Regularly monitor system performance and use insights to adapt strategies in real time.

Real-World Example

Ecosystems demonstrate natural flexibility. After a forest fire, plants adapted to fire-prone environments — such as fire-resistant trees or fast-growing grasses — quickly restore the ecosystem. This resilience stems from diversity and adaptability, ensuring that the system recovers even after significant disruption.

Why It Matters

Rigid systems are brittle, prone to collapse when conditions change. For example, companies that resist adopting new technologies often fall behind competitors who embrace innovation and adapt to evolving markets. Flexibility ensures that systems can pivot and thrive.

Flexibility also supports long-term sustainability. Systems designed to adapt are better equipped to handle ongoing challenges like climate change, economic instability, or population growth. For instance, cities with flexible zoning laws can adjust to changing needs, such as creating affordable housing during population surges.

Finally, enhancing flexibility fosters confidence and engagement. Stakeholders feel empowered when systems are adaptable and responsive, creating an environment of collaboration and innovation.

Exercises

1. **Identify a Rigid System:** Choose a system you interact with that struggles to adapt to change. What makes it rigid, and how could flexibility be introduced?

2. **Propose a Modular Design:** For a project or process, redesign it into smaller, independent parts that can be adjusted without disrupting the whole system.

3. **Test Flexibility:** Implement a small change in a system and observe how it adapts. Use the insights to improve its responsiveness to future challenges.

Key Takeaway

Flexibility ensures resilience. Systems that adapt to change are better equipped to thrive in dynamic environments.

Chapter 83: Seek Diversity for Stability

Strength in Variety

Diversity is a cornerstone of stability in systems. Whether in ecosystems, economies, or social structures, incorporating varied elements reduces reliance on any single component and creates resilience against disruptions. Diversity provides backup mechanisms, fosters innovation, and ensures that systems can adapt to change.

For example, ecosystems with diverse plant species are more resistant to pests and diseases than monocultures. If one species is affected, others can fill its role, maintaining ecosystem functions like nutrient cycling and soil stabilization. Similarly, organizations with diverse teams benefit from a broader range of perspectives, leading to creative problem-solving and better decision-making.

Seeking diversity isn't just about inclusion; it's about designing systems that are robust, flexible, and prepared to thrive under a wide range of conditions.

How to Seek Diversity

1. **Identify Vulnerabilities:** Look for areas in the system that rely heavily on a single resource, process, or perspective. These are points of fragility.

2. **Incorporate Multiple Elements:** Introduce varied components to reduce dependence on any one factor, such as diversifying suppliers, stakeholders, or approaches.

3. **Encourage Cross-Pollination:** Foster collaboration between different fields, industries, or disciplines to bring fresh ideas and solutions into the system.

4. **Monitor and Adjust:** Continuously evaluate whether diversity is improving resilience and adjust strategies as needed to address gaps or imbalances.

Real-World Example

In finance, diversified investment portfolios are a classic example of seeking diversity for stability. By spreading investments across different asset classes, sectors, and regions, investors reduce the risk of losses from any single market downturn, ensuring steadier overall performance.

Why It Matters

Homogeneity creates fragility. Systems that rely on a single crop, technology, or perspective are vulnerable to failure when conditions change. For instance, monoculture farming increases the risk of catastrophic crop failures due to pests or disease. In contrast, farms with diverse crops are more resilient and sustainable.

Diversity also fosters innovation. When systems integrate varied elements, they unlock new possibilities and solutions. For example, diverse teams in organizations consistently outperform homogeneous ones by bringing unique perspectives to problem-solving and decision-making.

Finally, seeking diversity supports equity and inclusion. Systems that embrace different voices and experiences are not only fairer but also better equipped to address the needs of all stakeholders.

Exercises

1. **Assess a System's Diversity:** Choose a system you interact with, such as a workplace, community, or project. Identify areas where diversity is strong and where it's lacking.

2. **Introduce Variety:** For a system you manage, propose ways to increase diversity, such as by adding new team members, strategies, or resources.

3. **Track Diversity's Impact:** Implement changes and monitor how increased diversity affects the system's stability, adaptability, or performance.

Key Takeaway

Diversity creates resilience. Incorporating varied elements strengthens systems and prepares them to thrive under changing conditions.

Chapter 84: Analyze Success Stories

Learning from What Works

Analyzing success stories offers valuable insights into what makes systems thrive. Whether it's a thriving ecosystem, a high-performing team, or a well-executed project, understanding why something worked reveals replicable practices and principles. This approach shifts the focus from merely solving problems to actively creating success.

For instance, Singapore's transformation from a resource-scarce city-state to a global economic hub is a success story built on strategic planning, innovation, and investment in human capital. By studying its journey, other cities can identify strategies like prioritizing education and fostering business-friendly policies to drive sustainable growth.

Success stories are more than inspiring — they provide blueprints for effective system design, revealing what aligns goals, resources, and processes to achieve exceptional outcomes.

How to Analyze Success Stories

1. **Select Relevant Examples:** Choose success stories similar to the system you're analyzing, ensuring their lessons are applicable to your context.

2. **Identify Key Drivers:** Focus on the factors that contributed most to the success, such as leadership, collaboration, or innovation.

3. **Extract Replicable Practices:** Highlight strategies or processes that can be adapted to your own system.

4. **Consider Contextual Factors:** Analyze what unique conditions or constraints shaped the success story and how they might differ from your own situation.

Real-World Example

Toyota's lean manufacturing system is a widely studied success story. Its focus on eliminating waste, improving efficiency, and empowering employees revolutionized the automotive industry. Organizations worldwide have adapted these principles — known as "lean thinking" — to enhance their operations, from healthcare to software development.

Why It Matters

Studying success shifts the narrative from problem-fixing to possibility-building. It provides practical insights into what works and why, helping systems move beyond survival toward thriving. For example, a non-profit studying a successful fundraising campaign can replicate strategies like personalized outreach or leveraging social media to achieve similar results.

Success stories also build confidence and momentum. Highlighting what's possible inspires teams and stakeholders to aim higher, fostering a culture of ambition and innovation.

Additionally, analyzing success uncovers transferable principles. Even if the exact context isn't replicable, the underlying strategies — such as prioritizing stakeholder engagement or leveraging technology — often apply across different systems.

Exercises

1. **Choose a Success Story:** Identify a system or project that succeeded in an area you're interested in. What made it effective?

2. **Extract Lessons:** Break down the success into key factors or strategies that contributed to its outcomes. How might you apply these lessons to your own system?

3. **Adapt and Test:** Implement one strategy from the success story in your context. Monitor its impact and refine it to fit your specific needs.

Key Takeaway

Success stories are blueprints for excellence — analyzing what works reveals lessons and practices that drive thriving systems.

Chapter 85: Foster Community-Led Solutions

Empowering Local Voices

Solutions that arise from within communities are often the most effective and sustainable. Community-led approaches leverage local knowledge, skills, and relationships to address challenges in ways that align with unique needs and contexts. This collaborative method not only creates practical solutions but also fosters a sense of ownership and empowerment among participants.

Consider participatory urban planning projects where local residents help design public spaces. In Medellín, Colombia, community involvement in transforming unsafe neighborhoods into vibrant areas with parks and libraries led to lasting change. Residents felt invested in the outcomes, ensuring the spaces were maintained and well-used.

Fostering community-led solutions shifts the focus from top-down interventions to bottom-up collaboration, ensuring that solutions resonate deeply with those they impact.

How to Foster Community-Led Solutions

1. **Engage Early and Often:** Involve community members from the start of the process, ensuring their voices shape both the goals and strategies.

2. **Leverage Local Knowledge:** Recognize and respect the expertise that communities have about their own challenges, resources, and dynamics.

3. **Facilitate Collaboration:** Provide platforms for dialogue and cooperation, where diverse stakeholders can share ideas, align efforts, and build trust.

4. **Support Capacity Building:** Equip communities with the tools, training, or resources they need to implement and sustain solutions.

Real-World Example

In Kenya, the M-Pesa mobile payment system emerged as a community-driven response to limited banking access. By addressing a local challenge with a solution tailored to the context, M-Pesa transformed financial inclusion for millions, becoming a global model for mobile banking.

Why It Matters

Community-led solutions ensure that interventions are practical and culturally appropriate. Top-down approaches often fail because they overlook local nuances or impose solutions that don't align with the community's reality. For example, international aid projects that ignore local customs may face resistance or inefficiencies, while those co-created with communities achieve greater acceptance and impact.

This approach also fosters resilience. When communities are empowered to solve their own challenges, they develop skills, networks, and confidence that prepare them to handle future issues independently.

Additionally, involving communities builds trust and accountability. People are more likely to support and sustain solutions they've had a hand in shaping, creating stronger and more cohesive systems.

Exercises

1. **Identify Community Assets:** Choose a community challenge and map its existing resources, skills, and networks. How might these be leveraged for solutions?

2. **Facilitate a Collaboration:** Organize a brainstorming session with diverse stakeholders to explore community-driven approaches to a local issue.

3. **Empower with Resources:** Design a plan to provide tools, training, or funding that supports a community in implementing its own solutions.

Key Takeaway

Community-led solutions align with local needs and foster empowerment. Collaborative approaches build trust, resilience, and long-term success.

Chapter 86: Identify Overlooked Costs

The Price You Don't See

In systems thinking, it's critical to recognize not just the obvious costs but also the overlooked ones — those that might not appear immediately but accumulate over time. Ignoring these hidden trade-offs often leads to inefficiencies, financial losses, or harm to stakeholders and the environment.

For instance, a company might cut costs by using cheaper materials, but the overlooked costs — product failures, loss of reputation, and warranty claims — outweigh the initial savings. Similarly, neglecting maintenance on infrastructure might save money in the short term but leads to far greater expenses when systems fail and require costly repairs.

Identifying overlooked costs ensures that decisions are made with a full understanding of their long-term impacts, avoiding pitfalls that could undermine the system's success.

How to Identify Overlooked Costs

1. **Consider Long-Term Impacts:** Analyze how decisions today might create expenses in the future, such as maintenance, resource depletion, or environmental harm.
2. **Assess Externalities:** Look for costs that might be shifted onto others, such as pollution affecting local communities or public health systems.
3. **Analyze Dependencies:** Recognize how decisions might strain other parts of the system, creating indirect costs like inefficiencies or delays.
4. **Involve Stakeholders:** Engage diverse perspectives to uncover costs that may not be immediately apparent from a single vantage point.

Real-World Example

Single-use plastics illustrate overlooked costs. While cheap and convenient, their environmental impact — including cleanup expenses, harm to marine life, and microplastic contamination — imposes massive costs on ecosystems and public health. Shifting to reusable materials addresses these hidden costs, promoting long-term sustainability.

Why It Matters

Overlooking costs often leads to short-sighted decisions that harm the system's resilience and sustainability. For example, companies that prioritize shareholder profits without investing in employee well-being often face high turnover rates, recruitment expenses, and productivity losses.

Accounting for all costs — visible and hidden — creates more balanced and sustainable strategies. For instance, renewable energy systems might seem costly upfront, but they eliminate long-term expenses associated with fossil fuel pollution, health impacts, and resource scarcity.

Additionally, identifying overlooked costs builds trust and accountability. Stakeholders are more likely to support decisions that consider broader impacts, ensuring equitable outcomes for all involved.

Exercises

1. **Analyze a Past Decision:** Reflect on a choice that seemed cost-effective initially but led to unexpected expenses later. What were the overlooked costs, and how could they have been accounted for?

2. **Map Externalities:** Choose a system or process and identify costs that might be shifted onto others, such as environmental or social impacts.

3. **Plan for Long-Term Costs:** For a current decision, outline potential hidden costs and propose strategies to address them upfront.

Key Takeaway

Overlooked costs undermine sustainability — recognizing them ensures balanced decisions that account for long-term impacts.

Chapter 87: Adapt to Changing Environments

New Challenges and Opportunities

Survival Through Adaptation

Change is inevitable, and systems that fail to adapt risk stagnation or collapse. Whether it's shifting market demands, evolving technologies, or environmental transformations, dynamic conditions require systems to adjust their processes, goals, and strategies. Adaptability isn't just about survival — it's about thriving in uncertainty and turning challenges into opportunities.

Take the retail industry, for example. Companies that quickly adapted to the rise of e-commerce, such as Amazon and Shopify, transformed their business models to meet changing consumer behaviors. Those that clung to traditional approaches struggled or disappeared. Adaptable systems recognize change as a constant and build mechanisms to respond flexibly.

By designing systems that evolve alongside their environments, you create resilience and ensure continued relevance, no matter how conditions shift.

How to Adapt to Changing Environments

1. **Monitor Trends:** Stay informed about external forces shaping the environment, such as technological advancements, social trends, or policy changes.
2. **Foster Agility:** Build systems that can pivot quickly, such as modular processes, cross-trained teams, or flexible technologies.
3. **Encourage Experimentation:** Test small changes to learn what works and scale successful strategies.
4. **Engage Stakeholders:** Involve diverse voices to anticipate changes from multiple perspectives and develop inclusive solutions.

Real-World Example

Netflix's evolution from DVD rentals to a streaming platform exemplifies adaptability. By recognizing the decline of physical media and the rise of online content, Netflix shifted its business model and pioneered an industry, staying ahead of competitors and maintaining its relevance.

Why It Matters

Failure to adapt often leads to irrelevance. For instance, Kodak, once a leader in photography, struggled to transition to digital technology, ultimately losing its market position to more adaptable competitors. Systems that anticipate and embrace change are better equipped to handle disruptions and seize emerging opportunities.

Adaptability also fosters innovation. As conditions change, new possibilities arise — whether through advancements in technology, shifts in consumer preferences, or environmental transformations. Adaptable systems harness these opportunities to grow and evolve.

Finally, adaptability ensures sustainability. Systems designed to evolve can respond to long-term challenges like climate change or population growth, creating solutions that endure over time.

Exercises

1. **Analyze Past Adaptation:** Reflect on a time when a system you were part of successfully adapted to change. What factors enabled this success?

2. **Anticipate Future Changes:** Identify trends or challenges that might affect a system you manage. How could you prepare to adapt to these changes?

3. **Design an Agile Strategy:** Choose a goal or process and outline steps to make it more adaptable, such as building in flexibility or testing new approaches.

Key Takeaway

Adaptability ensures resilience — systems that evolve alongside changing environments thrive in uncertainty and seize opportunities for growth.

Chapter 88: Optimize for Long-Term Outcomes

Thinking Beyond the Immediate

In a fast-paced world, it's tempting to focus on short-term goals — whether cutting costs, meeting deadlines, or achieving quick wins. However, optimizing for long-term outcomes creates stability, sustainability, and greater value over time. This approach requires balancing immediate needs with broader objectives, ensuring that actions today build a foundation for tomorrow.

For instance, investing in renewable energy infrastructure may be costly upfront, but it yields long-term benefits in reduced emissions, energy independence, and economic savings. Similarly, companies that prioritize employee development may see short-term costs but gain a loyal, skilled workforce that drives sustained success.

Optimizing for the long term means adopting a mindset of patience, planning, and purpose, ensuring that systems are designed to endure and thrive.

How to Optimize for Long-Term Outcomes

1. **Clarify Long-Term Goals:** Define what success looks like over years or decades, aligning actions with these objectives.

2. **Evaluate Trade-Offs:** Analyze how short-term decisions might impact long-term outcomes, ensuring that immediate benefits don't undermine sustainability.

3. **Invest Strategically:** Prioritize resources for initiatives that deliver enduring value, even if they require upfront sacrifices.

4. **Monitor Progress:** Regularly track how actions align with long-term goals, adjusting strategies to stay on course.

Real-World Example

The reforestation efforts in Costa Rica exemplify long-term thinking. By protecting forests and restoring degraded lands, the country has created sustainable ecosystems that support biodiversity, tourism, and climate resilience, proving that investments in the environment yield lasting benefits.

Why It Matters

Short-term thinking often creates inefficiencies and missed opportunities. For example, businesses that prioritize quarterly profits over long-term growth may underinvest in innovation, ultimately losing their competitive edge. Optimizing for long-term outcomes ensures that systems remain relevant and robust.

Long-term thinking also aligns with sustainability. Systems that consider future impacts, such as green infrastructure or education reform, address root causes rather than symptoms, creating solutions that endure.

Additionally, focusing on the long term builds trust. Stakeholders recognize and value organizations and systems that prioritize future well-being, fostering loyalty and collaboration.

Exercises

1. **Analyze a Short-Term Trade-Off:** Reflect on a recent decision that prioritized immediate results. How might a focus on long-term outcomes have changed the approach or results?

2. **Set a Long-Term Goal:** Choose a system or project and outline its desired outcomes over the next decade. What steps today will support these goals?

3. **Design for Endurance:** Propose a strategy to optimize a system for long-term success, such as investing in training, infrastructure, or sustainability initiatives.

Key Takeaway

Optimizing for long-term outcomes ensures sustainability and stability — decisions today build the foundation for success tomorrow.

Chapter 89: Create Sustainable Systems

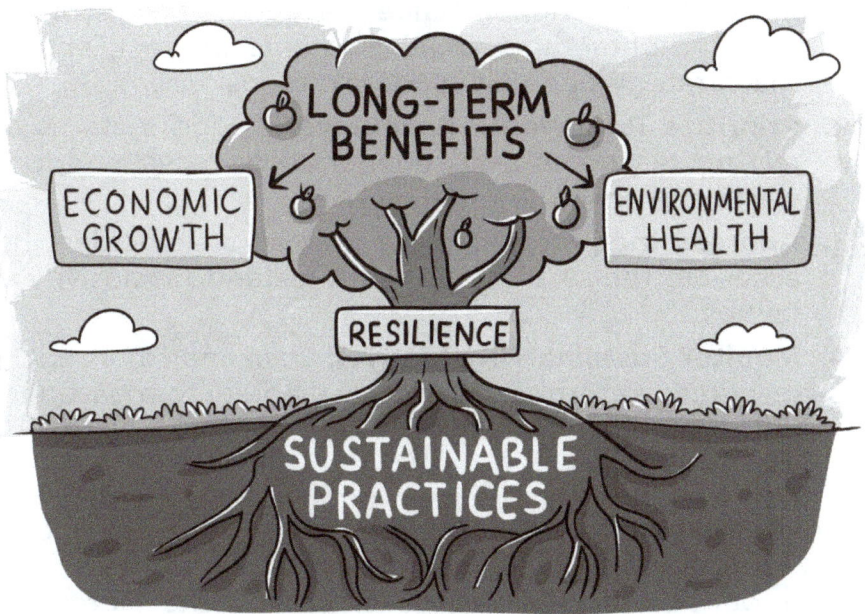

Building Systems That Endure

Sustainability ensures that systems can meet present needs without compromising the ability of future generations to thrive. It involves balancing economic, environmental, and social goals, recognizing their interconnections and mutual dependence. Sustainable systems prioritize longevity, resilience, and equity, creating value that extends far beyond immediate outcomes.

For example, Denmark's investment in wind energy demonstrates sustainability in action. By shifting to renewable energy, the country reduces its reliance on fossil fuels, protects the environment, and creates green jobs, achieving economic and ecological benefits simultaneously.

Creating sustainable systems requires intentional design, long-term thinking, and a commitment to adaptability.

Whether in urban planning, business strategy, or community development, sustainability offers a path to thriving in a resource-constrained world.

How to Create Sustainable Systems

1. **Integrate Interdependence:** Recognize how economic, environmental, and social elements interact, ensuring that strategies benefit all three dimensions.

2. **Prioritize Renewable Resources:** Design systems that rely on resources that regenerate or recycle, reducing waste and environmental harm.

3. **Address Inequities:** Ensure that all stakeholders have access to the system's benefits, fostering inclusivity and fairness.

4. **Monitor Sustainability Metrics:** Track indicators such as resource use, emissions, or social equity to measure and improve sustainability.

Real-World Example

The Netherlands' water management system is a global model of sustainability. By integrating ecological restoration, flood prevention, and urban development, the Dutch have created systems that protect communities while supporting biodiversity and tourism.

Why It Matters

Unsustainable systems create fragility and inequity. For example, overexploiting natural resources might boost profits temporarily but leads to environmental degradation, resource scarcity, and economic instability. Sustainable systems ensure that benefits endure across generations.

Sustainability also drives innovation. By addressing challenges like climate change or inequality, systems uncover new opportunities, such as green technologies or community-driven solutions. For example, companies investing in sustainable supply chains often gain competitive advantages in increasingly eco-conscious markets.

Finally, sustainable systems build trust. When stakeholders see a commitment to long-term well-being, they're more likely to engage, support, and collaborate, creating a virtuous cycle of growth and stability.

Exercises

1. **Evaluate a System:** Choose a system you're part of and assess its sustainability in terms of economic, environmental, and social dimensions. What improvements could make it more balanced?

2. **Propose a Sustainable Initiative:** Design a project or policy that prioritizes long-term sustainability, such as a renewable energy program or community-based recycling effort.

3. **Track Metrics:** Implement your initiative and monitor its sustainability indicators. Reflect on lessons learned and potential refinements.

Key Takeaway

Sustainable systems balance economic, environmental, and social goals. Intentional design ensures longevity and thriving across generations.

Chapter 90: Incorporate Circular Economy Principles

Closing the Loop

A circular economy replaces the traditional "take-make-waste" model with one that keeps resources in use for as long as possible. By designing products, processes, and systems to minimize waste and maximize reuse, circular economies create value while reducing environmental impact.

For instance, Patagonia, the outdoor clothing company, incorporates circular economy principles by offering repair services, recycling old garments, and creating products from recycled materials. This approach not only reduces waste but also strengthens customer loyalty and brand identity.

Incorporating circular economy principles requires rethinking how resources flow through systems. It's about designing for regeneration, ensuring that nothing is wasted and everything has a purpose.

How to Incorporate Circular Economy Principles

1. **Design for Longevity:** Create products and systems that last longer, with components that are easy to repair, upgrade, or reuse.
2. **Minimize Waste:** Identify points where resources are discarded and redesign processes to capture and reuse them.
3. **Promote Sharing and Reuse:** Encourage models like sharing platforms or product-as-a-service to maximize resource efficiency.
4. **Close Material Loops:** Ensure that materials are recycled or composted back into the system, reducing dependence on virgin resources.

Real-World Example

In Sweden, a "recycling revolution" has led to only 1% of household waste being sent to landfills. Through rigorous recycling, waste-to-energy programs, and public engagement, Sweden has become a global leader in closing material loops and reducing environmental impact.

Why It Matters

Linear systems that rely on extracting resources and discarding waste are inherently unsustainable. They deplete finite materials, pollute ecosystems, and create economic inefficiencies. Circular economies address these issues by keeping resources in use, reducing environmental harm, and creating economic opportunities.

Circular systems also drive innovation. By rethinking traditional processes, businesses and communities uncover new ways to create value, such as developing biodegradable packaging or using waste as raw material for new products.

Finally, circular economy principles align with societal shifts toward sustainability. As consumers increasingly demand eco-friendly options, organizations that embrace circular models position themselves as leaders in a changing market.

Exercises

1. **Identify Waste in a System:** Choose a system or process you're familiar with and map points where resources are wasted. How could these materials be reused or recycled?

2. **Design a Circular Product:** Develop a concept for a product or service that incorporates circular economy principles, such as durability, repairability, or recyclability.

3. **Promote Circular Practices:** Create a plan to implement circular practices in a community or workplace, such as a composting program or material-sharing initiative.

Key Takeaway

Circular economies create value by keeping resources in use. Incorporating these principles reduces waste and builds sustainable systems.

Chapter 91: Match Innovation with Stability

Balancing Change and Continuity

Innovation drives progress, but without stability, it can disrupt systems or lead to unsustainable growth. Stability provides the foundation that allows innovation to flourish without causing chaos. Matching these two forces creates systems that are dynamic yet dependable, capable of evolving while maintaining their core functions.

Consider the renewable energy sector. While innovation has led to breakthroughs like solar panels and wind turbines, stable infrastructure — such as reliable grids and storage solutions — ensures that these technologies integrate seamlessly into existing energy systems. The balance allows for progress without risking blackouts or inefficiencies.

By aligning innovation with stability, you can create systems that adapt to new challenges and opportunities while preserving the structures that sustain them.

How to Match Innovation with Stability

1. **Identify Core Functions:** Define which parts of the system must remain stable to ensure reliability, such as essential services, processes, or values.

2. **Encourage Experimentation:** Create space for testing and adopting innovative ideas without disrupting the system's foundation.

3. **Develop Supportive Structures:** Ensure that stable processes, resources, or policies enable innovation to thrive without causing imbalance.

4. **Monitor System Dynamics:** Regularly assess how innovation and stability interact, making adjustments to maintain balance.

Real-World Example

The automotive industry demonstrates this balance. Electric vehicle (EV) manufacturers innovate with battery technologies and autonomous driving, while stable supply chains and manufacturing standards ensure consistent quality and reliability. Together, these forces drive progress without sacrificing trust or functionality.

Why It Matters

Innovation without stability leads to fragility. For example, start-ups that scale too quickly often collapse under the weight of insufficient processes or resources. Stability ensures that systems can absorb and sustain growth.

On the other hand, stability without innovation fosters stagnation. Organizations or systems that resist change risk becoming obsolete, as seen in industries that fail to adapt to technological advancements. Matching stability with innovation ensures continued relevance and resilience.

This balance also builds stakeholder confidence. Stable systems that embrace change demonstrate reliability and forward-thinking, fostering trust among investors, employees, and communities.

Exercises

1. **Analyze a System:** Identify a system you're part of, such as a workplace or community. Are innovation and stability balanced, or does one dominate?

2. **Propose a Balanced Strategy:** Design an approach to integrate a new idea or technology while maintaining the system's essential functions.

3. **Evaluate Progress:** Implement your strategy and track how the balance between innovation and stability affects the system's performance.

Key Takeaway

Innovation and stability are complementary forces. Aligning them creates systems that evolve while maintaining resilience and reliability.

Chapter 92: Focus on Interdependence

Everything is Connected

Interdependence lies at the heart of systems thinking. No element of a system operates in isolation — each is connected to and influenced by others. Recognizing and strengthening these connections ensures that systems function cohesively, adapt to change, and achieve shared goals.

For example, sustainable agriculture depends on healthy ecosystems, economic viability, and social support. Farmers need fertile soil (environment), fair prices (economy), and community cooperation (social systems). When these elements work together, the entire system thrives. Ignoring one weakens the others, leading to instability.

Focusing on interdependence means designing systems where connections are acknowledged, nurtured, and leveraged to create positive feedback and resilience.

How to Focus on Interdependence

1. **Map Relationships:** Identify how elements within the system are connected, such as dependencies between stakeholders, processes, or resources.

2. **Strengthen Links:** Build bridges between disconnected or weakly connected parts of the system, fostering collaboration and coordination.

3. **Align Goals:** Ensure that different components of the system work toward shared objectives, reducing conflict and inefficiency.

4. **Monitor Changes:** Continuously evaluate how shifts in one part of the system affect others, adjusting strategies as needed.

Real-World Example

The One Health approach to global health recognizes the interdependence of human, animal, and environmental health. By addressing these areas collectively — such as combating zoonotic diseases or promoting sustainable farming — this approach creates solutions that benefit all interconnected systems.

Why It Matters

Ignoring interdependence often leads to unintended consequences. For instance, deforestation might provide short-term economic gains but disrupt ecosystems, water cycles, and local communities, causing long-term harm. Recognizing these connections ensures balanced decisions.

Focusing on interdependence also fosters collaboration. When systems are designed to align efforts, such as government agencies working with businesses and non-profits, they achieve more cohesive and impactful results.

Finally, interdependence enhances resilience. Well-connected systems distribute resources, knowledge, and support, making them better equipped to handle disruptions or crises.

Exercises

1. **Identify Interdependencies:** Choose a system you interact with and create a diagram of how its elements connect. Reflect on how strengthening these links could improve performance.
2. **Analyze a Disruption:** Think of a time when one part of a system failed. How did it affect other components, and what could have minimized the impact?
3. **Design Collaborative Solutions:** Propose a strategy that leverages interdependence to address a challenge, such as creating partnerships or integrating processes.

Key Takeaway

Interdependence is the foundation of system health. Acknowledging and strengthening connections ensures cohesive, resilient systems.

Chapter 93: Address Core Problems

Digging Deep

In complex systems, it's easy to get caught up addressing surface-level symptoms, such as inefficiencies or recurring crises. However, these are often signals of deeper issues — core problems rooted in the system's structure or design. Addressing core problems directly leads to more sustainable and impactful solutions, preventing the same symptoms from re-emerging.

For example, addressing traffic congestion by expanding roads might temporarily reduce delays but often worsens the problem through induced demand. The core problem—lack of public transportation or overreliance on cars—remains unaddressed. Shifting focus to developing efficient public transit systems or walkable cities tackles the root cause, creating long-term solutions.

By identifying and solving core problems, you reduce waste, frustration, and inefficiency, building systems that operate smoothly and effectively.

How to Address Core Problems

1. **Trace Symptoms to Causes:** Use tools such as root-cause analysis to uncover the underlying issues driving surface-level problems.

2. **Examine System Structure:** Identify elements like feedback cycles, bottlenecks, or imbalances that perpetuate core problems.

3. **Prioritize Impactful Solutions:** Focus on interventions that address root causes rather than quick fixes for symptoms.

4. **Involve Stakeholders:** Collaborate with those affected to ensure the core problem is accurately identified and the solution is widely supported.

Real-World Example

The Flint water crisis highlighted the danger of addressing symptoms without tackling core problems. Short-term solutions, such as switching water sources, failed to address systemic issues like infrastructure neglect and inadequate oversight. Only by focusing on these root causes can sustainable solutions for clean, safe water be achieved.

Why It Matters

Focusing on symptoms creates inefficiencies and wastes resources. For instance, repeatedly patching a leaking pipe without replacing it leads to ongoing costs and disruptions. Tackling the core issue—replacing outdated infrastructure — provides a lasting fix.

Addressing core problems also prevents cascading failures. In ecosystems, ignoring issues like habitat destruction can lead to widespread consequences, from species extinction to climate instability. Solving root causes stabilizes the entire system.

Finally, targeting core problems fosters innovation and resilience. Solutions that address foundational issues often unlock new opportunities for growth and collaboration, strengthening the system as a whole.

1. **Trace a Problem's Roots:** Choose a recurring issue in a system you interact with and analyze its root causes. What structural factors or feedback loops sustain it?

2. **Propose a Core Solution:** Design an intervention that addresses the root cause of the problem. How would this approach prevent symptoms from recurring?

3. **Monitor Impact:** Implement your solution and track how effectively it eliminates symptoms. Reflect on lessons learned and potential refinements.

Key Takeaway

Sustainable solutions focus on core problems — addressing root causes builds efficient, resilient systems that prevent recurring issues.

Chapter 94: Simplify Complex Systems

The Elegance of Simplicity

Complex systems can be overwhelming, with layers of processes, stakeholders, and interdependencies. While some complexity is inherent and necessary, much of it stems from inefficiencies, outdated practices, or unclear priorities. Simplifying systems allows you to focus on critical components, improving efficiency, clarity, and adaptability.

Consider healthcare systems burdened by excessive administrative processes. Streamlining patient records, automating repetitive tasks, and reducing bureaucratic hurdles frees up resources for direct patient care, improving outcomes and efficiency.

Simplification doesn't mean oversimplifying — it's about removing unnecessary complications while retaining the system's essential functions and goals.

How to Simplify Complex Systems

1. **Identify Key Components:** Distinguish between essential and nonessential elements, focusing on what drives the system's core functions.

2. **Streamline Processes:** Eliminate redundancies, bottlenecks, or unnecessary steps that slow the system down.

3. **Use Clear Communication:** Standardize language, formats, or tools to ensure that all stakeholders understand the system's goals and operations.

4. **Test for Efficiency:** Implement changes incrementally, evaluating how each adjustment improves clarity or performance.

Real-World Example

The Kanban method, used in manufacturing and project management, simplifies workflows by visualizing tasks on a board. This approach helps teams identify priorities, track progress, and reduce inefficiencies, making complex projects more manageable and transparent.

Why It Matters

Unnecessary complexity creates frustration and inefficiency. For example, complicated tax codes confuse taxpayers and increase compliance costs. Simplifying forms and processes improves accessibility and reduces errors.

Simplified systems are also more adaptable. When external conditions change, streamlined structures can pivot more easily than cumbersome, overly layered ones. For instance, businesses with clear decision-making processes adjust more quickly to market shifts than those bogged down by excessive approvals.

Finally, simplification fosters collaboration. Clear, well-organized systems make it easier for stakeholders to engage, share insights, and align efforts, enhancing overall performance.

Exercises

1. **Map a Complex System:** Choose a system you interact with and create a diagram of its components. Identify areas where complexity could be reduced.

2. **Propose Simplifications:** Suggest changes to streamline processes, such as removing redundancies or standardizing communication tools.

3. **Evaluate Simplification's Impact:** Implement your proposed changes and monitor how they affect the system's efficiency and effectiveness.

Key Takeaway

Simplifying complex systems enhances clarity, efficiency, and adaptability. Focusing on essentials ensures sustainable and effective performance.

Chapter 95: Develop Systemic Thinking Habits

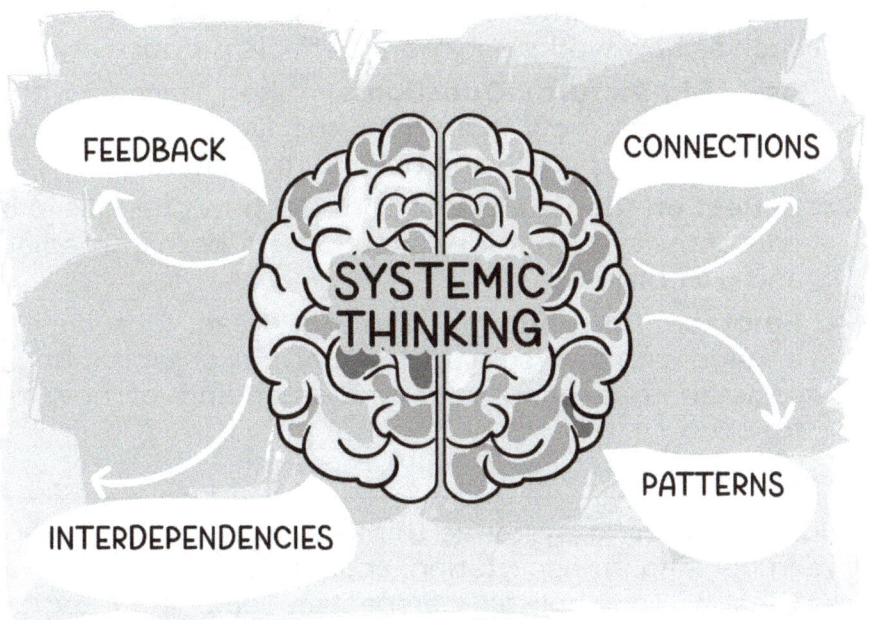

Cultivating a Systems Mindset

Systems thinking isn't just a tool; it's a habit — a way of seeing and understanding the world. Developing systemic thinking habits involves training your mind to recognize patterns, connections, and interdependencies in everyday situations. This mindset transforms how you approach problems, plan solutions, and navigate complexity.

For instance, a teacher using systemic thinking might not only focus on individual student performance but also consider factors like classroom dynamics, family support, and curriculum design. By addressing these interconnected elements, the teacher creates a more supportive and effective learning environment.

Making systems thinking a habit requires practice, curiosity, and a commitment to looking beyond the surface. Over time, this approach becomes second nature, enabling you to make smarter, more informed decisions.

How to Develop Systemic Thinking Habits

1. **Practice Seeing Connections:** Regularly map out how different elements in a situation influence one another, such as how workplace morale affects productivity.
2. **Ask Big-Picture Questions:** When faced with a problem, ask how it fits into the larger system. What forces are shaping it, and how do they interact?
3. **Reflect on Ripple Effects:** Consider how changes in one part of the system might affect others, both immediately and over time.
4. **Embrace Continuous Learning:** Read, observe, and engage with diverse systems—natural, organizational, or societal—to expand your understanding of how they function.

Real-World Example

In urban planning, systemic thinkers consider the interplay between housing, transportation, economic opportunities, and public health. This holistic perspective leads to integrated solutions, such as mixed-use developments that reduce commuting times while promoting community well-being.

Why It Matters

Systemic thinking habits enhance problem-solving by encouraging you to look beyond symptoms and address root causes. For example, a company facing high turnover might initially focus on salary adjustments but discover, through systemic analysis, that workplace culture or career development opportunities are the real drivers.

These habits also improve collaboration. Understanding interconnections fosters empathy and alignment, helping teams and stakeholders work together toward shared goals.

Finally, systemic thinking builds adaptability. By recognizing patterns and feedback loops, you can anticipate challenges and design solutions that evolve alongside changing conditions.

Exercises

1. **Daily Connections Practice:** Each day, pick a situation or problem and identify at least three interconnected elements that influence it. Reflect on how they shape the outcome.

2. **Unpack a Recent Decision:** Think of a decision you made recently and diagram its ripple effects across different parts of the system. What insights emerge?

3. **Engage in Systems Learning:** Explore a system outside your expertise, such as an ecosystem or an economic model. What connections and patterns do you notice?

Key Takeaway

Developing systemic thinking habits transforms how you understand and navigate complexity. Consistent practice makes this perspective second nature.

Chapter 96: Use Systems Thinking in Policy

Policies That Work Holistically

Effective policy design requires more than addressing immediate problems. It demands a systems-thinking approach. Policies impact multiple areas simultaneously, creating ripple effects that shape communities, economies, and environments. Systems thinking ensures that these interconnections are acknowledged, aligned, and leveraged for maximum benefit.

For example, policies promoting renewable energy not only reduce carbon emissions but also create jobs, improve public health, and strengthen energy independence. A systems-thinking approach integrates these benefits into a comprehensive strategy that maximizes positive outcomes.

Using systems thinking in policy means crafting solutions that are sustainable, equitable, and adaptable. This holistic perspective avoids unintended consequences and ensures that policies serve the needs of diverse stakeholders.

How to Use Systems Thinking in Policy

1. **Map Policy Interconnections:** Identify how a proposed policy affects different systems and stakeholders, including potential indirect impacts.

2. **Anticipate Ripple Effects:** Analyze how changes in one area — such as education reform — might influence related areas like workforce readiness or economic growth.

3. **Engage Stakeholders:** Involve diverse voices in the policymaking process to uncover blind spots and ensure that policies address multiple perspectives.

4. **Monitor and Adapt:** Continuously evaluate the impact of policies, making adjustments to address emerging challenges or opportunities.

Real-World Example

Finland's education policies demonstrate systemic thinking. By focusing on teacher training, equitable funding, and holistic curricula, Finland has built a system where education excellence supports broader social and economic outcomes, such as reduced inequality and high innovation rates.

Why It Matters

Policies designed without systems thinking often produce unintended consequences. For instance, agricultural subsidies that incentivize monoculture farming may boost short-term yields but lead to long-term environmental degradation and reduced biodiversity. Systems thinking ensures that policies consider both immediate and downstream effects.

This approach also fosters alignment between policy goals. For example, policies addressing housing affordability can integrate public transportation and green infrastructure, creating synergies that enhance quality of life while reducing carbon footprints.

Finally, systems-thinking policies build resilience. By considering how policies interact with dynamic environments, they remain effective even as conditions change, ensuring sustained impact.

1. **Analyze a Policy:** Choose a policy you're familiar with and outline its impacts on different systems. What interconnections and ripple effects do you observe?

2. **Propose a Holistic Policy:** Design a policy that addresses a key issue while supporting multiple goals, such as economic growth, sustainability, and public health.

3. **Evaluate Policy Outcomes:** Select an existing policy and assess how well it aligns with systems-thinking principles. What changes could improve its effectiveness?

Key Takeaway

Systems thinking creates policies that are holistic, sustainable, and resilient — aligning diverse goals ensures long-term success.

Chapter 97: Challenge Default Mental Models

Reframing the Way You See Systems

Default mental models are the ingrained assumptions and frameworks people use to understand the world. While they provide shortcuts for decision-making, these models often limit perspectives, reinforce biases, and oversimplify complexity. Challenging these default assumptions is essential for effective systems thinking, as it opens up new possibilities and prevents flawed decisions.

For example, many organizations operate under the assumption that profit maximization is the sole measure of success. Challenging this mental model reveals alternative approaches, such as focusing on social impact, sustainability, or stakeholder well-being, which can lead to more balanced and enduring success.

By questioning default mental models, you uncover hidden assumptions, expand your understanding, and design solutions that align with the true dynamics of a system.

How to Challenge Default Mental Models

1. **Identify Assumptions:** Reflect on the beliefs and frameworks you use to interpret a situation. What do you take for granted?

2. **Consider Alternatives:** Explore other ways of understanding the system, drawing on diverse perspectives, disciplines, or data sources.

3. **Engage in Critical Reflection:** Ask probing questions like, "What if this assumption is wrong?" or "What am I missing?" to uncover blind spots.

4. **Test New Models:** Experiment with alternative mental models and evaluate how they affect your understanding and decision-making.

Real-World Example

In the energy sector, the default mental model that fossil fuels were the only viable source of energy dominated for decades. Challenging this assumption led to breakthroughs in renewable energy, like solar and wind, reshaping global energy systems and addressing environmental challenges.

Why It Matters

Default mental models can perpetuate systemic problems. For instance, the assumption that economic growth must come at the expense of environmental health has driven unsustainable practices. Challenging this model reveals opportunities for green growth and circular economies.

Reframing mental models also drives innovation. By questioning "the way things have always been done," systems become more open to novel ideas, partnerships, and strategies. For example, ride-sharing services like Uber and Lyft emerged by challenging the traditional taxi model.

Finally, breaking free from default assumptions fosters inclusivity. By considering diverse perspectives, systems are better equipped to serve a wider range of stakeholders, creating more equitable outcomes.

Exercises

1. **Identify a Default Model:** Think of a mental model you commonly use, such as "Success equals profit." Reflect on how this assumption shapes your decisions.

2. **Reframe the Model:** Explore alternative perspectives. For example, how might success be measured in terms of social impact or resilience?

3. **Test a New Approach:** Apply an alternative mental model to a decision or problem and evaluate the results. How did this shift in perspective affect outcomes?

Key Takeaway

Challenging default mental models reveals hidden assumptions and unlocks new possibilities. This practice expands understanding and drives better decisions.

Chapter 98: Invest in Continuous Learning

Staying Curious in a Changing World

Continuous learning is the foundation of effective systems thinking. As systems evolve, new challenges and opportunities arise, requiring a mindset of curiosity and adaptability. Investing in ongoing learning ensures that you remain responsive to change, deepen your understanding, and refine your strategies over time.

For example, in the fast-changing field of technology, professionals who prioritize continuous learning —by attending workshops, pursuing certifications, or engaging in peer learning — stay ahead of industry shifts, ensuring their relevance and success.

Continuous learning isn't limited to formal education. It includes seeking feedback, reflecting on experiences, and engaging with diverse perspectives to uncover new insights and refine your approach to complex systems.

How to Invest in Continuous Learning

1. **Adopt a Growth Mindset:** View challenges and mistakes as opportunities to learn and grow rather than as setbacks.

2. **Engage in Lifelong Education:** Pursue formal and informal learning opportunities, such as courses, books, podcasts, or mentoring relationships.

3. **Reflect on Experiences:** Regularly analyze past actions and outcomes to identify lessons and apply them moving forward.

4. **Learn from Others:** Seek out diverse perspectives and collaborate with people from different disciplines, backgrounds, or industries.

Real-World Example

The Japanese concept of Kaizen, or continuous improvement, embodies the value of ongoing learning. Companies like Toyota use Kaizen to refine processes and products incrementally, creating a culture of innovation and excellence that has sustained their global success.

Why It Matters

Without continuous learning, systems stagnate. For instance, businesses that resist adapting to new technologies or market trends often lose relevance, while those that invest in learning thrive in dynamic environments.

Continuous learning also builds resilience. As new challenges arise — such as climate change or technological disruptions — learning equips systems with the knowledge and tools needed to adapt effectively.

Finally, lifelong learning fosters collaboration. Engaging with diverse ideas and perspectives creates opportunities for innovation and alignment, strengthening systems and their outcomes.

Exercises

1. **Reflect on Past Lessons:** Identify a recent challenge or success and analyze what you learned from it. How can you apply these lessons moving forward?

2. **Pursue a Learning Opportunity:** Choose a topic or skill you're curious about and explore resources like books, courses, or mentorships to deepen your knowledge.

3. **Collaborate for Growth:** Join a discussion group or network with people outside your field to exchange insights and expand your perspective.

Key Takeaway

Continuous learning ensures adaptability and growth. Staying curious and open equips systems to thrive in dynamic environments.

Chapter 99: Empower the Marginalized

Inclusion is Strength

Empowering marginalized voices is not just a moral imperative — it's essential for system health and resilience. Marginalized individuals and groups often experience first-hand the consequences of system inefficiencies, inequities, or blind spots, giving them unique insights into problems and potential solutions. Bringing these voices into the conversation enriches decision-making, strengthens collaboration, and ensures that systems are more inclusive and effective.

For example, Indigenous communities have long been stewards of their environments, using traditional knowledge to maintain ecological balance. Empowering these voices in modern conservation efforts bridges scientific and cultural approaches, creating sustainable solutions that honor both innovation and tradition.

Empowerment goes beyond inviting participation — it involves redistributing power, providing resources, and fostering environments where diverse perspectives can thrive and shape systems meaningfully.

How to Empower the Marginalized

1. **Identify Barriers:** Analyze systemic obstacles that prevent marginalized groups from participating fully, such as unequal access to education, technology, or decision-making platforms.

2. **Create Opportunities:** Design programs, policies, or initiatives that actively include marginalized voices and prioritize their leadership.

3. **Redistribute Resources:** Ensure equitable access to tools, funding, and networks needed for meaningful participation.

4. **Foster Representation:** Amplify the voices of underrepresented groups through mentorship, advocacy, or community-led initiatives.

Real-World Example

In Brazil, marginalized communities in the Amazon rainforest have been empowered through partnerships with conservation organizations. These collaborations prioritize Indigenous leadership in forest protection, combining local knowledge with global resources to address deforestation and climate change.

Why It Matters

Ignoring marginalized voices perpetuates inequity and inefficiency. For instance, urban planning projects that exclude low-income residents often result in gentrification, displacement, and social fragmentation. Empowering these communities ensures solutions are inclusive and equitable.

This approach also strengthens systems. Diverse perspectives challenge default assumptions, drive innovation, and create outcomes that work for a broader range of stakeholders.

Finally, empowerment builds trust and solidarity. When marginalized groups see their contributions valued, it fosters collaboration and a shared commitment to system-wide success.

Exercises

1. **Identify Marginalized Voices:** In a system you're part of, reflect on which groups are underrepresented. What barriers prevent their participation?

2. **Design an Empowerment Strategy:** Develop an initiative to amplify marginalized voices, such as through mentorship, resource distribution, or collaborative decision-making.

3. **Evaluate Inclusivity:** Assess the impact of your strategy on the system's inclusivity and effectiveness. What lessons emerge for future efforts?

Key Takeaway

Empowering marginalized voices enriches systems. This approach ensures equity, drives innovation, and strengthens collective success.

Chapter 100: Apply Systems Thinking Everywhere

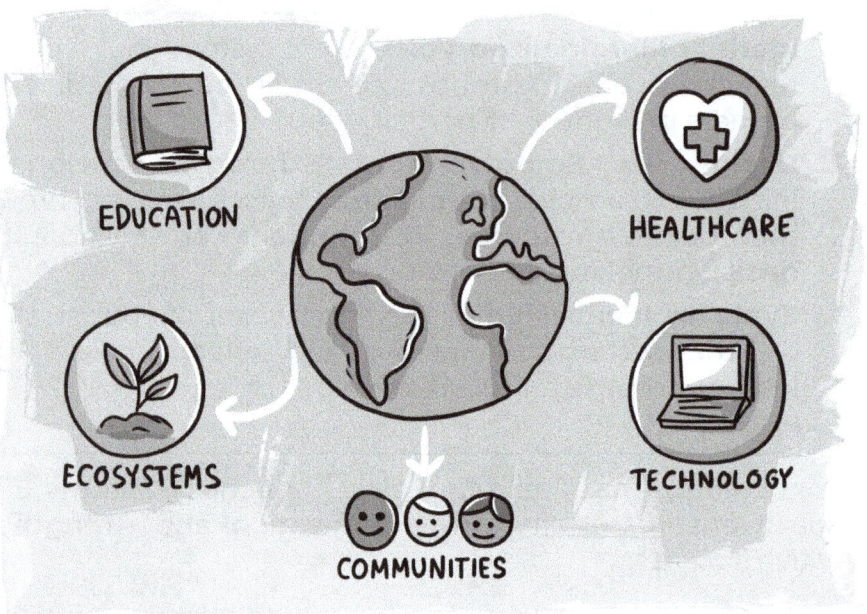

A Universal Lens

Systems thinking isn't limited to specific fields or industries. it's a universal framework for understanding and navigating the interconnectedness of life. Whether you're managing a household, leading an organization, or addressing global challenges, systems thinking offers tools to uncover relationships, anticipate outcomes, and design solutions that align with larger goals.

For instance, applying systems thinking in personal finance involves not just budgeting but also considering long-term goals, external economic factors, and interdependencies like family needs or career growth. In this context, it ensures more thoughtful and sustainable decision-making.

By applying systems thinking everywhere, you cultivate a habit of seeing beyond surface-level problems, fostering a mindset that values connection, adaptability, and purpose in every aspect of life.

How to Apply Systems Thinking Everywhere

1. **Adopt a Systems Perspective Daily:** Reflect on how your actions and decisions connect to larger systems, whether in relationships, work, or community involvement.

2. **Start Small:** Practice systems thinking on everyday challenges, such as organizing a team project or managing personal routines.

3. **Expand Gradually:** Apply these principles to more complex systems, like organizational strategies, community initiatives, or global issues.

4. **Teach and Share:** Empower others to embrace systems thinking by modeling the approach, sharing insights, and fostering collaborative problem-solving.

Real-World Example

The Global Vaccine Alliance (Gavi) applies systems thinking to improve access to vaccines worldwide. By addressing interconnected factors like supply chains, healthcare infrastructure, and public education, Gavi creates scalable and sustainable solutions that save lives.

Why It Matters

Applying systems thinking universally transforms how people approach challenges. It shifts the focus from isolated fixes to integrated solutions, creating lasting impact across diverse domains.

This approach also fosters global resilience. In a world of interconnected crises — such as climate change, pandemics, and economic instability — systems thinking provides a roadmap for navigating complexity and driving collective progress.

Finally, systems thinking enriches personal growth. By viewing yourself as part of larger networks, you gain deeper awareness of your role, purpose, and potential to contribute meaningfully to the world.

Exercises

1. **Start with an Everyday System:** Choose a simple system in your life, such as meal planning or commuting. How can systems thinking improve its efficiency or impact?

2. **Apply to a Broader Context:** Identify a larger system—such as a workplace or community initiative—and map its connections. What insights emerge?

3. **Share Your Insights:** Teach a friend, colleague, or family member one principle of systems thinking and discuss how it applies to their experiences.

Key Takeaway

Systems thinking is a universal tool. Applying it everywhere unlocks new perspectives and creates meaningful impact in every facet of life.

Conclusion: The Transformative Power of Systems Thinking

As you reach the final pages of this book, reflect on the journey you've undertaken. You've explored 100 ways to uncover connections, anticipate ripple effects, and design solutions that align with the deeper dynamics of the systems around you. This is more than just a set of tools—it's a transformative perspective that redefines how you approach problems, opportunities, and change.

Valuable Learnings

The practical insights in this book has equipped you to:

- **Spot Interconnections:** See the relationships between seemingly unrelated parts, helping you identify leverage points and design more impactful solutions.

- **Address Root Causes:** Move beyond treating symptoms to tackle the foundational issues driving system behaviors.

- **Foster Resilience:** Design systems that adapt to change, recover from disruptions, and thrive in complexity.

- **Collaborate Inclusively:** Recognize and integrate diverse voices to create solutions that are equitable, innovative, and enduring.

- **Balance Short-Term and Long-Term Goals:** Navigate the tension between immediate needs and sustainable outcomes with clarity and purpose.

These skills are universally applicable, empowering you to tackle challenges in personal life, professional settings, communities, and global contexts.

Practical Tips for Applying Systems Thinking

1. **Start Small:** Practice systems thinking on manageable challenges, such as improving team workflows, optimizing a personal project, or streamlining household routines. Identify interconnections and experiment with small changes to observe their impact.

2. **Define Relationships:** Use tools like mind maps, diagrams, or even simple lists to visualize how the parts of a system interact. This exercise reveals dependencies, bottlenecks, and opportunities for intervention.

3. **Ask Questions:** Develop the habit of asking systems-oriented questions: What are the ripple effects? Who or what else is affected? What feedback loops are at play?

4. **Think Across Time Scales:** When making decisions, consider both short-term benefits and long-term consequences. For instance, investing in employee training might reduce immediate output but create lasting gains in productivity and morale.

5. **Involve Others:** Systems thrive on collaboration. Share what you've learned, invite diverse perspectives, and work with stakeholders to co-create solutions that benefit the broader network.

6. **Stay Curious:** Systems are dynamic. Keep learning by observing natural systems, studying successful models, or exploring new frameworks. Continuous curiosity fuels your ability to adapt and innovate.

Moving Forward

Systems thinking isn't a skill you master overnight; it's a lifelong practice. Each system you engage with offers new lessons, challenges, and opportunities for growth. Embrace this mindset in all areas of your life — at home, at work, and in the world.

The true power of systems thinking lies in its ability to bridge gaps. It connects the micro and the macro, the present and the future, the individual and the collective. When applied thoughtfully, it fosters solutions that are as inclusive as they are effective, creating value for yourself and the systems you inhabit.

Now, the responsibility shifts to you. Use the insights from this book to inspire change, build resilience, and create a positive impact. Whether you're redesigning a workflow, addressing community challenges, or tackling global issues, remember: no action is too small when it's part of a larger, interconnected whole.

Appendix A: Chapter Summaries

This appendix serves as your quick-reference guide to the 100 chapters of this book. Each chapter title is accompanied by a brief description of its key idea, allowing you to revisit concepts, refresh your understanding, or find inspiration as you apply systems thinking in your life.

Part 1: The Basics of Seeing Systems (Chapters 1–20)

1. **Zoom Out to See the Big Picture**

   Recognize how stepping back reveals patterns that are not immediately visible.

2. **Identify Key Stakeholders**

   Visualize who is affected by and influences the system.

3. **Trace Causal Links**

   Follow the chain of events to find the root causes driving system behaviors.

4. **Spot Feedback Loops**

   Detect reinforcing cycles in the system.

5. **Unpack Delay Dynamics**

   Recognize where time lags disrupt relationships.

6. **Look for System Boundaries**

   Define where a system starts and ends for clarity.

7. **Observe Resource Flows**

   Track how energy, materials, or money move through the system.

8. **Notice Points of Tension**

Detect areas where competing forces create instability.

9. **Uncover Emergent Behavior**

See how simple interactions create complex outcomes.

10. **Understand System History**

Study the past to explain present system behavior.

11. **Visualize Interconnections**

Use diagrams to reveal relationships between system parts.

12. **Distinguish Stocks from Flows**

Separate accumulations (stocks) from changes (flows).

13. **Notice Self-Organization**

Observe how systems structure themselves without external control.

14. **Focus On Tipping Points**

Identify thresholds where small changes create large effects.

15. **See Patterns Across Scales**

Look for recurring behaviors at micro, macro, and in-between levels.

16. **Look for Missing Connections**

Identify gaps where elements should interact but don't.

17. **Assess System Resilience**

Evaluate how well a system recovers from disruptions.

18. **Find Balancing Forces**

Recognize what stabilizes or restrains growth in the system.

19. **See Dependencies**

Trace how one part of the system relies on another.

20. **Recognize How Systems Change**

Notice how systems adjust in response to internal or external pressures.

Part 2: Analyzing Human-Created Systems (Chapters 21–40)

21. Study Incentive Structures

Identify rewards and penalties driving behavior in the system.

22. Watch out for Backfiring Motivators

Identify cases where rewards unintentionally cause harm or undesired outcomes.

23. Track Decision Pathways

Follow how choices propagate through the system.

24. Examine Rules and Norms

Understand formal and informal guidelines shaping interactions.

25. Map Communication Channels

See how information flows influence outcomes.

26. Notice Bottlenecks

Find points where flows slow down or get stuck.

27. Identify System Archetypes

Pinpoint recurring structures such as "Success to the Successful" that shape system behavior.

28. Explore Power Bases

Spot who has control and how they use it.

29. Find Leverage Points

Locate small changes that yield big results.

30. Trace Resource Inequalities

Observe how uneven distributions create systemic issues.

31. Spot Structural Biases

Identify embedded advantages or disadvantages in the system.

32. Understand The Snowball Effect

Explore how small changes can lead to major outcomes.

33. Analyze Network Centrality

Study which nodes or actors are most influential.

34. Look for Cross-System Overlaps

Notice when systems share characteristics.

35. Track Failures to Learn

Examine breakdowns to understand vulnerabilities.

36. Identify Siloed Thinking

Spot isolated parts that limit broader coordination.

37. Evaluate the Role of Middle Actors

Observe intermediaries that mediate connections or flows.

38. See Intermediary Goals

Notice how mid-level objectives shape larger outcomes.

39. Spot the Pace of Change

Assess whether the system evolves too quickly or slowly for its environment.

40. Detect Systemic Fragility

Recognize when a system is too rigid to adapt.

Part 3: Spotting Patterns in Natural Systems (Chapters 41–60)

41. See Cycles Everywhere

Identify recurring natural rhythms like seasons or migrations.

42. Understand Energy Flows

Follow how energy moves through ecosystems.

43. Uncover Predator-Prey Dynamics

Observe how nature's relationships are intertwined.

44. Trace Nutrient Paths

Study how elements like carbon and nitrogen circulate.

45. Find Anchor Points

Discover the critical species or elements that have an outsized impact on the system's stability.

46. Notice Niche Functions

Discover how unique functions contribute to the stability and success of a system.

47. Evaluate Mechanisms

Study how ecosystems bounce back after disruption.

48. Find Cascading Effects

Observe how small ecological shifts ripple through the system.

49. Detect Resource Competition

Watch how organisms or groups vie for limited supplies.

50. Observe Natural "Evolution"

See how changes in behavior or structure meet evolving needs.

51. Recognize Interconnected Ecosystems

Understand how forests, oceans, and rivers rely on each other.

52. Spot Self-Healing Solutions

Study how damaged environments recover naturally.

53. See Nature's Redundancies

Observe backups that provide support in critical areas.

54. Trace Habitat Fragmentation

Follow how breaking habitats affects broader systems.

55. Watch Energy Minimization Strategies

Observe how natural systems optimize efficiency.

56. Look for Mutualism

Study win-win relationships in ecosystems.

57. Detect Adaptive Behaviors

See how ecosystems grow, collapse, and renew over time.

58. Understand Biotic-Abiotic Interactions

Study how living organisms affect non-living elements and vice versa.

59. See Human-Nature Interactions

Explore how humans impact and are shaped by natural systems.

60. Track Species Migration Networks

Follow the dynamic flows of populations over time.

Part 4: Applying Systems Thinking to Solve Problems (Chapters 61–100)

61. Break Down the Problem into Subsystems

Dissect challenges into manageable, interrelated parts.

62. Use Feedback for Continuous Improvement

Adjust actions based on real-time results.

63. Test Small Interventions

Experiment in a controlled way to learn before scaling.

64. Activate Unused Resources

Identify overlooked assets within the system.

65. Find Nonlinear Influences

Spot where small shifts create unpredictable changes.

66. Build Strong Systems

Design for flexibility and recovery from shocks.

67. Eliminate Obstructions

Free up critical choke points.

68. Encourage Cross-System Collaboration

Connect isolated parts to solve shared problems.

69. Monitor Leading Indicators

Track early signs of upcoming changes.

70. Avoid Over-Optimization

Prevent pushing efficiency to the point of fragility.

71. Develop Iterative Solutions

Tweak and improve systems in cycles.

72. Align Incentives

Adjust motivations to drive system-wide benefits.

73. Broaden Your Scope of Analysis

Include external factors that influence the system's behavior.

74. Reduce Delays in Reporting

Shorten loops for faster, more accurate adjustments.

75. **Encourage Transparency**
Make flows and connections within the system clear and easy to understand.

76. **Counteract Perverse Incentives**
Reframe goals to align actions with desired outcomes.

77. **Use Systems Thinking in Leadership**
Lead teams with a holistic, interconnected perspective.

78. **Apply Risk Management Systems**
Anticipate and mitigate potential disruptions.

79. **Strengthen Weak Connections**
Fortify the most vulnerable parts of a system.

80. **Design for Redundancy**
Add backups to critical parts for longevity.

81. **Avoid Unintended Consequences**
Predict and address secondary effects of changes.

82. **Enhance System Flexibility**
Build the ability to adapt to unexpected shifts.

83. **Seek Diversity for Stability**
Integrate varied elements for robustness.

84. **Analyze Success Stories**
Learn from systems that thrive.

85. **Foster Community-Led Solutions**
Empower local stakeholders to drive change.

86. **Identify Overlooked Costs**
Spot trade-offs that may not be immediately apparent in decisions.

87. **Adapt to Changing Environments**
Align systems with shifting external conditions.

88. **Optimize for Long-Term Outcomes**
Balance immediate gains with future needs.

89. **Create Sustainable Systems**
Design processes that maintain equilibrium.

90. Incorporate Circular Economy Principles

Close loops to reuse resources effectively.

91. Match Innovation with Stability

Introduce change without destabilizing the system.

92. Focus on Interdependence

Strengthen connections that boost overall health.

93. Address Core Problems

Go beyond just looking at symptoms, aim to find solutions.

94. Simplify Complex Systems

Streamline without losing essential functions.

95. Develop Systemic Thinking Habits

Practice spotting connections in everyday life.

96. Use Systems Thinking in Policy

Shape laws with an understanding of ripple effects.

97. Challenge Default Mental Models

Question assumptions to see systems differently.

98. Invest in Continuous Learning

Build capacity to remain flexible as systems evolve.

99. Empower the Marginalized

Bring overlooked voices into systemic change.

100. Apply Systems Thinking Everywhere

Recognize that no part of life exists in isolation.

Appendix B: Section and Chapter Guide

This appendix organizes the book by its four main sections and chapters. It's designed to help you quickly locate topics of interest and see how the book's structure builds from foundational concepts to advanced applications.

The Basics of Seeing Systems

- Zoom Out to See the Big Picture
- Identify Key Stakeholders
- Trace Causal Links
- Spot Feedback Loops
- Unpack Delay Dynamics
- Look for System Boundaries
- Observe Resource Flows
- Notice Points of Tension
- Uncover Emergent Behavior
- Understand System History
- Visualize Interconnections
- Distinguish Stocks from Flows
- Notice Self-Organization
- Focus On Tipping Points
- See Patterns Across Scales
- Look for Missing Connections

- Assess System Resilience
- Find Balancing Forces
- See Dependencies
- Recognize How Systems Change

Analyzing Human-Created Systems

- Study Incentive Structures
- Watch out for Backfiring Motivators
- Track Decision Pathways
- Examine Rules and Norms
- Map Communication Channels
- Notice Bottlenecks
- Identify System Archetypes
- Explore Power Bases
- Find Leverage Points
- Trace Resource Inequalities
- Spot Structural Biases
- Understand The Snowball Effect
- Analyze Network Centrality
- Look for Cross-System Overlaps
- Track Failures to Learn
- Identify Siloed Thinking
- Evaluate the Role of Middle Actors
- See Intermediary Goals
- Spot the Pace of Change
- Detect Systemic Fragility

Spotting Patterns in Natural Systems

- See Cycles Everywhere
- Understand Energy Flows
- Uncover Predator-Prey Dynamics
- Trace Nutrient Paths
- Find Anchor Points

- Notice Niche Functions
- Evaluate Mechanisms
- Find Cascading Effects
- Detect Resource Competition
- Observe Natural "Evolution"
- Recognize Interconnected Ecosystems
- Spot Self-Healing Solutions
- See Nature's Redundancies
- Trace Habitat Fragmentation
- Watch Energy Minimization Strategies
- Look for Mutualism
- Detect Adaptive Behaviors
- Understand Biotic-Abiotic Interactions
- See Human-Nature Interactions
- Track Species Migration Networks

Applying Systems Thinking to Solve Problems

- Break Down the Problem into Subsystems
- Use Feedback for Continuous Improvement
- Test Small Interventions
- Activate Unused Resources
- Find Nonlinear Influences
- Build Strong Systems
- Eliminate Obstructions
- Encourage Cross-System Collaboration
- Monitor Leading Indicators
- Avoid Over-Optimization
- Develop Iterative Solutions
- Align Incentives
- Broaden Your Scope of Analysis
- Reduce Delays in Reporting
- Encourage Transparency
- Counteract Perverse Incentives

- Use Systems Thinking in Leadership
- Apply Risk Management Systems
- Strengthen Weak Connections
- Design for Redundancy
- Avoid Unintended Consequences
- Enhance System Flexibility
- Seek Diversity for Stability
- Analyze Success Stories
- Foster Community-Led Solutions
- Identify Overlooked Costs
- Adapt to Changing Environments
- Optimize for Long-Term Outcomes
- Create Sustainable Systems
- Incorporate Circular Economy Principles
- Match Innovation with Stability
- Focus on Interdependence
- Address Core Problems
- Simplify Complex Systems
- Develop Systemic Thinking Habits
- Use Systems Thinking in Policy
- Challenge Default Mental Models
- Invest in Continuous Learning
- Empower the Marginalized
- Apply Systems Thinking Everywhere

Appendix C: Practice Scenarios

This appendix is designed to help you apply the principles of systems thinking to real-world situations. Each scenario presents a system-related problem, followed by a challenge that prompts you to think critically about how to use the concepts and strategies from this book. These exercises will help solidify your understanding of systems thinking and build confidence in your ability to navigate complex challenges.

Scenario 1: Traffic Congestion in a Growing City

Problem: A rapidly growing city is experiencing severe traffic congestion during peak hours. Expanding roads temporarily relieved the issue but has worsened it over time due to increased car usage. Public transportation options are limited and underfunded.

Challenge: Apply the principles of **"Find Leverage Points" (Chapter 29)** and **"Address Core Problems" (Chapter 93)** to identify the root causes of congestion and propose a long-term solution that reduces reliance on personal vehicles.

Scenario 2: Declining Team Productivity

Problem: A project team's productivity has been steadily declining. Team members report unclear goals, miscommunication, and bottlenecks in decision-making. Morale is low, and deadlines are being missed.

Challenge: Use **"Map Communication Channels" (Chapter 25)** and **"Strengthen Weak Connections" (Chapter 79)** to identify how information flows and interpersonal relationships can be improved to boost productivity and morale.

Scenario 3: Community Water Shortages

Problem: A rural community is facing seasonal water shortages due to overuse and inefficient irrigation practices. Efforts to dig new wells have not addressed the underlying issue, and tensions between farmers and residents are growing.

Challenge: Leverage **"Observe Resource Flows" (Chapter 7)** and **"Develop Systemic Thinking Habits" (Chapter 95)** to track water use and design a sustainable water management system that balances agricultural and residential needs.

Scenario 4: Declining Pollinator Populations

Problem: A region has seen a sharp decline in pollinator species, threatening local agriculture. While some farmers have switched to artificial pollination methods, these are expensive and less effective.

Challenge: Use **"Find Anchor Points" (Chapter 45)** and **"Look for Mutualism" (Chapter 56)** to identify critical relationships in the ecosystem and propose strategies to restore pollinator populations naturally.

Scenario 5: Siloed Departments in an Organization

Problem: Departments in a company operate in silos, leading to inefficiencies and duplicated efforts. Employees feel isolated, and innovation is stifled due to a lack of cross-departmental collaboration.

Challenge: Apply **"Identify Siloed Thinking" (Chapter 36)** and **"Encourage Cross-System Collaboration" (Chapter 68)** to design initiatives that break down silos and promote interdepartmental cooperation.

Scenario 6: Housing Shortages in Urban Areas

Problem: Urban housing shortages are driving up rents and displacing lower-income residents. Developers are hesitant to build affordable housing due to low profit margins, exacerbating the issue.

Challenge: Use **"Trace Resource Inequalities" (Chapter 30)** and **"Analyze Success Stories" (Chapter 84)** to address the systemic causes of housing shortages and propose policies that incentivize equitable development.

Scenario 7: Overreliance on a Single Supplier

Problem: A manufacturing company depends heavily on a single supplier for critical components. A recent disruption in the supplier's operations caused costly delays and missed production deadlines.

Challenge: Apply **"Diversify Resources" (Chapter 82)** and **"Strengthen Weak Connections" (Chapter 79)** to develop a more resilient supply chain.

Scenario 8: Persistent Classroom Disruptions

Problem: A teacher struggles to maintain order in a classroom where frequent disruptions undermine learning. Efforts to address individual students' behavior haven't resolved the broader problem.

Challenge: Use **"Notice Points of Tension" (Chapter 8)** and **"Uncover Emergent Behavior" (Chapter 9)** to identify systemic causes of the disruptions and propose strategies to create a supportive learning environment.

Scenario 9: Unequal Access to Healthcare

Problem: A rural area experiences unequal access to healthcare, with residents facing long travel distances and limited availability of medical professionals. Existing facilities are overwhelmed.

Challenge: Leverage **"Spot Structural Biases" (Chapter 31)** and **"Design for Redundancy" (Chapter 80)** to create a more equitable and robust healthcare delivery system.

Scenario 10: Overcrowded Public Transportation

Problem: A city's public transportation system is overcrowded and underfunded. Riders experience frequent delays, and complaints are rising, yet investment in infrastructure is stagnant.

Challenge: Apply **"Monitor Leading Indicators" (Chapter 69)** and **"Evaluate the Role of Middle Actors" (Chapter 37)** to identify solutions that improve service and secure stakeholder support for long-term investment.

Scenario 11: Low Employee Retention

Problem: A company struggles to retain employees, with high turnover resulting in increased hiring and training costs. Exit interviews reveal dissatisfaction with workplace culture and lack of career growth opportunities.

Challenge: Use **"Align Incentives" (Chapter 72)** and **"Analyze Network Centrality" (Chapter 33)** to create a workplace environment that motivates and retains talent.

Scenario 12: Food Waste in Supply Chains

Problem: A food retailer experiences high levels of waste, with unsold products often discarded due to spoilage. Supply chain inefficiencies and demand forecasting errors exacerbate the issue.

Challenge: Leverage **"Track Failures to Learn" (Chapter 35)** and **"Simplify Complex Systems" (Chapter 94)** to design a more efficient and sustainable supply chain.

Scenario 13: Lack of Disaster Preparedness

Problem: A coastal town faces recurring flooding but lacks adequate disaster preparedness. Past efforts to build infrastructure have been reactive rather than proactive.

Challenge: Use **"Enhance System Flexibility" (Chapter 82)** and **"Focus on Tipping Points" (Chapter 14)** to create a disaster management plan that builds long-term resilience.

Scenario 14: Low Community Engagement

Problem: A town struggles with low turnout for public meetings and a lack of participation in civic initiatives, leaving decisions to a small group of stakeholders.

Challenge: Apply **"Foster Community-Led Solutions" (Chapter 85)** and **"Encourage Transparency" (Chapter 75)** to design strategies that increase community engagement and trust.

Scenario 15: Inefficiencies in Resource Allocation

Problem: A non-profit organization struggles to allocate resources effectively, with some programs overfunded while others are chronically under-resourced.

Challenge: Leverage **"Observe Resource Flows" (Chapter 7)** and **"Find Leverage Points" (Chapter 29)** to optimize resource allocation and improve impact across all programs.

Appendix D: Your Checklist for Spotting Connections

This checklist is your quick-reference guide for integrating systems thinking into your daily life, work, and problem-solving. Each point distills key principles and strategies from the book into actionable steps, ensuring that you can apply what you've learned with ease and confidence. Use this checklist as a starting point for analyzing challenges, designing solutions, and fostering systemic change.

1. Zoom Out for the Big Picture

- Step back and identify the broader system influencing the situation.
- Look for patterns, trends, or connections that aren't immediately visible.
- Ask: "How does this fit into the larger context?"

2. Identify Key Stakeholders

- Visualize who is affected by the system and who influences it.
- Consider perspectives from diverse groups, including marginalized voices.
- Ask: "Whose input is missing, and how can I include it?"

3. Trace Root Causes

- Look beyond surface-level symptoms to uncover underlying problems.

- Use tools like root-cause analysis to connect symptoms to systemic issues.
- Ask: "What is driving this problem, and where does it originate?"

4. Map System Interconnections
- Create diagrams to visualize how elements within a system interact.
- Highlight dependencies, feedback loops, and points of tension.
- Use the map to identify opportunities for intervention or improvement.

5. Leverage Feedback Mechanisms
- Look for reinforcing or balancing cycles within the system.
- Identify areas where small changes can have significant ripple effects.
- Monitor feedback to adjust and refine your approach.

6. Address Bottlenecks
- Identify areas where flows or processes are slowed or blocked.
- Evaluate whether resources, time, or communication are contributing factors.
- Propose solutions to free up bottlenecks and restore efficiency.

7. Monitor Long-Term Impacts
- Assess how today's decisions will affect the system in the future.
- Balance short-term gains with long-term sustainability.
- Ask: "What are the unintended consequences of this action?"

8. Embrace Diversity in Systems
- Include diverse elements, perspectives, and resources to increase resilience.
- Recognize the value of redundancy and backup systems.

- Ask: "What variety does this system need to thrive?"

9. Strengthen Weak Connections

- Identify and fortify vulnerable links within the system.
- Foster collaboration and communication to bridge gaps.
- Ask: "Where is the system weakest, and how can I support it?"

10. Simplify Complexity

- Remove unnecessary steps or redundancies that hinder performance.
- Focus on essential goals and processes to improve clarity.
- Test simplifications incrementally to ensure they enhance effectiveness.

11. Foster Community-Led Solutions

- Empower stakeholders to design and implement solutions.
- Build trust through transparency, shared ownership, and collaboration.
- Provide tools, training, or resources to support their efforts.

12. Design for Flexibility

- Build systems that can adapt to changing conditions or disruptions.
- Use modular components to make adjustments easier.
- Monitor performance and adjust strategies based on feedback.

13. Anticipate Trade-Offs

- Evaluate the costs and benefits of each decision across different areas.
- Look for hidden costs that might emerge over time.
- Ensure that trade-offs align with long-term system goals.

14. Balance Innovation with Stability

- Foster creative thinking while maintaining reliable processes.
- Experiment in controlled ways that don't disrupt core functions.
- Regularly evaluate whether innovation and stability are aligned.

15. Keep Learning and Adapting

- Stay curious and open to new ideas, perspectives, and methods.
- Reflect on successes and failures to refine your approach.
- Engage with diverse systems to expand your understanding and skills.

Pro Tip

Systems thinking is a practice, not a destination. As you apply these principles, remember to stay adaptable, reflective, and patient. Start small, experiment, and learn from every experience. The more you practice, the easier it becomes to see connections, anticipate ripple effects, and design solutions that truly make a difference. Stay curious — the systems around you are waiting to teach you something new!

Here's another book by Quinn Voss that you might like

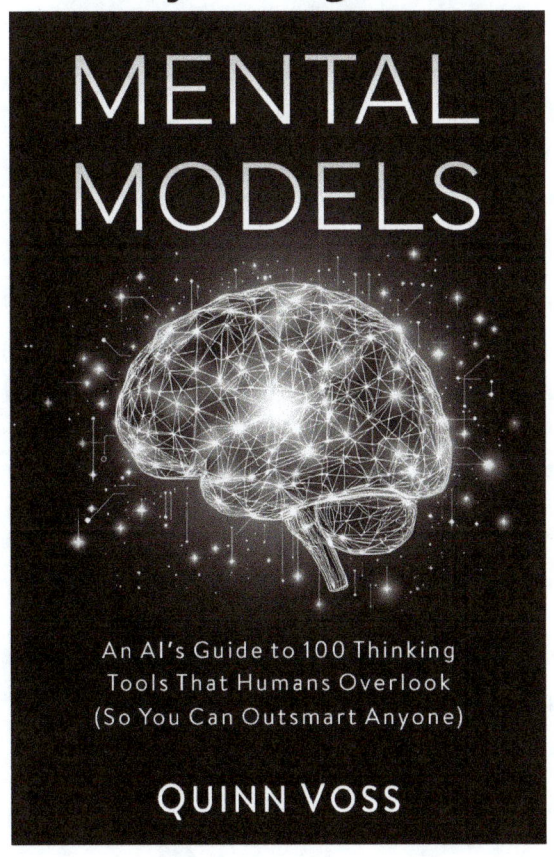

www.ingramcontent.com/pod-product-compliance
Lightning Source LLC
Chambersburg PA
CBHW061555120626
46550CB00004B/1492